WOMEN IN CHINA

WOMEN IN CHINA
KATIE CURTIN

PATHFINDER PRESS, NEW YORK AND TORONTO

Library of Congress Catalog Card Number 74-14166
ISBN 0-87348-404-5 (Cloth); 0-87348-405-3 (Paper)
Manufactured in the United States of America
Published in the United States by Pathfinder Press, Inc., New York and simultaneously in Canada by Pathfinder Press, Ltd., Toronto

First Edition, 1975

PATHFINDER PRESS, INC.
410 West Street
New York, N.Y. 10014

"The changes in a historical epoch may always be inferred from the comparative freedom of women in one part or another, for in an improvement in the relations between women and men, between the weak and the strong, we see most clearly the victory of human nature over the nature of the brute. . . . The degree of the emancipation of women is a natural standard of the general emancipation."

Karl Marx and Frederick Engels in *The Holy Family*

CONTENTS

WOMEN'S POSITION
IN THE OLD SOCIETY

In 1949 the Maoist peasant armies routed the troops of the Chiang Kai-shek dictatorship and wrenched China out of the grip of Western imperialism. In the years to come the new Communist Party regime would uproot the wealthy landlords, destroy the oppressive institutions that survived from China's precapitalist past, and finally, after some hesitation, abolish private capitalist ownership of factories. The creation of a planned, nationalized economy after 1953 opened the path to rapid improvement in the standard of living of the Chinese masses and giant strides forward. The revolution swept away the grinding poverty of the past, the threat of starvation, opium addiction, foreign domination.

This tremendous revolutionary upheaval led to radical changes in the family structure and in the status of women as well. Hundreds of thousands and even millions of women participated in the Chinese revolution, seeing in it the means for their emancipation. To what degree have Chinese women been freed from their traditional inferior status?

Any serious assessment of the progress of women's emancipation under the Maoist regime must begin with the conditions women faced in prerevolutionary China.

9

It has been said that Confucius, whose epigrams codi-
fied the ethics of precapitalist China, had not one favorable word for women. In traditional Chinese cosmology
the world was composed of two complementary elements:
The *yin,* the female, stood for all things dark, weak, and
passive; the *yang,* the male, for all things bright, strong,
and active.

Women's status was little better than a slave's. It was
said that women passed through three ages: In the first
she was under the authority of the father, then under her
husband, and finally, if he died, she was subject to her
son. Female infanticide was common, especially among
the lower classes: Not only was a female child an ex-
pense to raise, but later she needed a dowry to marry,
and her most productive years were devoted to the service not of her own but of her husband's family.

The binding of women's feet, introduced throughout
China in the tenth century, was seen as a mark of gentili-
ty and was most prevalent among the upper classes. This
barbarous custom was romanticized and eulogized but
its essential function was voiced in the old Chinese proverb, "Feet are bound, not to make them beautiful as a
curved bow, but to restrain women when they go out of
doors." The binding process, which had to be begun in
early childhood, was excruciatingly painful and ended
in permanent crippling. An idea of the deformity footbinding produced can be gained from comparing the
length of your own foot to the standard of perfect beauty
called the "Golden Lily" — a foot reduced to three inches
in length from heel to toe!

Marriages were not based on love or even mutual con-
sent. Rather they were arranged by the parents through
matchmakers. Often the couple had never laid eyes on
each other before the wedding day. After the marriage,
the husband-wife relationship was considered subordinate and supplementary to the parent-son relationship.

Because of a rule against marrying a person of the
same surname, marriage often meant the complete up-

rooting of the wife from her family, friends, and surroundings. John Lossing Buck studied a Chinese village in the 1920s and found that while 97 percent of the farm operators and 94 percent of their fathers had been born in the village, only 6.6 percent of their wives had been. [1]

A woman's role in life was to bear male children to perpetuate the family name and aid in the work. If she did not fulfill this task, she could be cast out of her husband's home, disgraced, and socially ostracized. It was only in her function as a breeder that she attained status in society. While a man could take additional wives, a woman could have only one husband. Widows were not allowed to remarry. Infidelity, tolerated and even encouraged in men, was social suicide for a woman.

"A woman married is like a pony bought — to be ridden or whipped at the master's pleasure." This proverb cogently sums up women's degraded marital status.

Some male writers have claimed that rather than being chattel, Chinese women really held the power. Dr. Hu Shih, one of China's foremost liberal philosophers and scholars during the first half of this century, was an exponent of this theory. He wrote that woman had always been the greatest despot of the family and that no other country could compete with China for its number of henpecked husbands. This refrain has been repeated many times and in many countries to try and mask women's inferior social status. While Chinese women in their capacities as mothers and mothers-in-law did hold some power, this was only over the women of the family; all the women still remained subordinate to the men. Occasionally a very strong woman would gain considerable control in her family, including over male members. But the real levers of power were held by the men, in the patriarchal male clan institutions of the village, and in the government bureaucracy. Women lacked legal and property rights and their only political influence lay in their ability to manipulate kinsmen.

Poor peasant women of necessity had to take part in production, which exempted them from footbinding. But unmarried daughters could still be sold by their fathers as concubines or prostitutes, and the custom of child brides was more prevalent among the rural poor than among richer classes.

The large extended family was not the norm among the poor. Contrary to popular myth, the average size of households in China was approximately five persons. The large joint family, with several generations under one roof, was an ideal that only the richer classes could afford.[2]

The poor peasant seldom could support more than one wife, while rich peasants and local lords had as many as they could afford. The richest of the local lords often had numerous wives, concubines, and slave girls from whom they benefitted both for their sexual pleasure and through labor in domestic industry. The local lord also used the many sons that issued from these unions as the basis for his political machine.[3]

In addition to his own wives and concubines, the rich landlord could also prey on the peasant women, especially the wives of his tenant farmers. Often the tenant and his wife would acquiesce out of fear of the consequences of refusal. But even if they protested, they had little chance to make the protest effective.

In *China Shakes the World,* Jack Belden described one such incident. In a western Shantung village there was a landlord who commonly went into the fields and raped the wife of his tenant, a peasant named Li. "When Li protested, the landlord had him kidnapped by bandits. In order to cover his participation in the kidnapping, the landlord pretended to mediate the affair through puppet troops, preparing a banquet on the tenant's behalf. . . . The grateful tenant was released and borrowed money from the kindly landlord to pay for the banquet. Of course, a high interest rate was charged, the tenant could not repay his debt, and lost his own small plot of ground. The landlord then consummated the whole affair by taking the tenant's wife as payment of the debt." 4

Besides class differences in the status of women, there were also regional differences. The conditions of women in North China, the old heartland of the dynastic imperial system, were more oppressive than in the South. There were deep prejudices in the North against women working in the fields, while it was acceptable practice in the South.

Despite the severe oppression of women, there were individuals who managed to make their mark in history. There were celebrated and educated women, usually daughters of scholars, who were taught to read and write by their families and were given a humanist education. There was a tradition of women writing poetry. During the reign of China's last dynasty alone, the Ch'ing or Manchu dynasty (1644-1911 AD), almost one thousand women left poetry in print. Some of the courtesans, who weren't bound by the same rules as most women, became known for their poetry, music, painting, and wit. 5

Despite the achievements of these individuals, however, the lot of women was one of subjection and suffering, frustrated dreams and unrealized potential.

How sad it is to be a woman!
Nothing on earth is held so cheap.
Boys stand leaning at the door
Like Gods fallen out of heaven.
Their hearts brave the Four Oceans,
The wind and dust of a thousand miles.
No one is glad when a girl is born;
By her the family sets no store.
(Fu Hsuan)

These oppressive patriarchal relations were first shaken in the penetration of China by Western imperialism in the nineteenth century. With the growth of industry there was a rapid increase in the urban population. Removed from the stifling atmosphere of the clan-dominated villages, many of the old customs became difficult to enforce. Moreover, the penetration of foreign capital began to convert the rural areas to production for the market and break down the traditional self-sufficiency of the village. One result was the accumulation of capital by the landlords and the growth of indebtedness on the part of the poor peasantry, with the result that there was a great increase in landless tenant farmers at the end of the nineteenth and beginning of the twentieth centuries. This tended also to reduce the size of rural families and drive the unemployed or underemployed youth into the urban centers in search of work.

The need for a cheap source of labor in the industrializing port cities led to the employment of female workers. Footbinding, which hindered women's participation in industry, began to be met with rising opposition, even within sectors of the ruling class. Educational opportunities for women began to open up, and while these were limited to a tiny percentage of the population, the example of emancipated women and the ideas they transmitted to others had an impact far beyond the numbers involved.

Urban working women, with their new financial contribution to the family, acquired a greater voice in family affairs. Able to support themselves economically, these Chinese women had new alternatives, including the possibility of terminating a marriage gone sour.

Chinese women have a history of struggling for their rights that extends back into the nineteenth century. In the Taiping rebellions from 1850 to 1865, women fought in women's brigades of the militia. The Taipings, who were fighting to overthrow the Ch'ing dynasty and establish a new, Taiping ("great peace") dynasty, called for an end to polygamy, slavery, adultery, and footbinding in their program. In 1853 the Taipings captured Nanking and made it their capital. In the first years of their rule they enacted some reforms for women. Later, however, polygamy and concubinage became prevalent in the courts of Taiping rulers.[6]

In the early nineteenth century an organized movement against marriage developed among women in the Shun-te district of Kwangtung. Many women in this district, mainly workers in the silk industry, refused to marry, remained virgins, and went to live in "Girls' Homes," where they stayed with others who shared their views. The movement, called "Girls Who Do Not Go to the Family," became so widespread that Kwantung authorities were forced to establish special homes for these women. This movement still existed in the late 1930s.[7]

THE EARLY WOMEN'S MOVEMENT

The imperialist penetration of China brought with it the ideas of bourgeois-democracy, which began to erode the cruder forms of precapitalist oppression of women. In the late 1800s the idea of female equality was championed by prominent liberal male reformers such as Liang Ch'i-ch'ao and K'an Yu-wei. These two proposed important changes in this area in the "hundred days" of sweeping reforms they persuaded the emperor to undertake in 1898. But these were abrogated by the Dowager Empress Tz'u-hsi who seized the throne to protect the old system.

Shortly after this, the first independent women leaders appeared on the scene. One of the most interesting was Ch'iu Chin. This brilliant and forceful woman was born into a scholarly family in 1875 and was educated in the classics, history, and poetry. She was profoundly influenced by the 1898 reform movement and became a women's rights advocate.

Unhappy in an arranged marriage, Ch'iu left her family and went to Japan to continue her studies. There she attended a teachers college and became active in revolutionary groups, joining the Encompassing Love Society (Kung-ai hu), a society of female progressives.

16

In her spare time she studied marksmanship and bombmaking.

In 1906 Ch'iu returned to Shanghai and joined the Restoration Society, the main revolutionary group in Kiangsu and Chekiang provinces. She served as headmistress of a women's modern middle school and also taught at a boys' school. Among the subjects she taught her pupils was military tactics.

In 1907 Ch'iu established China's first feminist newspaper. But later that year she was executed by the authorities after an attempt to assassinate a provincial governor and organize an armed insurrection in the schools failed.[8] In the 1911 revolution, however, her students formed a paramilitary brigade.

Young women were an important part of the revolutionary movement against the imperial dynasty. In Canton thousands of female students joined the 1908 patriotic demonstrations, and when the revolution against the imperial system broke out in 1911, girl students waged a struggle for the right to fight. Many joined women's brigades of the decentralized women's armies. In some areas women won the right to participate in the new provincial governments. After the establishment of the republic in 1912, however, the women's army was disbanded because the new government found the military wing of the women's rights movement too threatening.[9]

One woman prominent in the women's brigades was Sophia Chang, a leader of the Revolutionary Alliance. She had taken the name "Sophia" in honor of Sophia Pirovskaya, one of the women who participated in the assassination of Tsar Alexander II. Chang, a Shanghai schoolteacher, organized women there in support of the revolution, raising funds through performances of plays dealing with the American, French, and Chinese revolutions.

When the republic was established in 1912, a group of women's organizations petitioned the Provisional Parliament demanding that the new constitution grant equal rights to women. When they were ignored, young women physically stormed the Parliament, breaking its windows and injuring guards.

China broke up into a number of warlord states after the 1912 revolution. In the course of this development the women's movement was crushed. For seven years little activity was seen in this sphere. [10]

But although the scope of activity greatly diminished, it did not stop altogether. In 1916 the newly established Chinese Renaissance movement leveled powerful ideological attacks on the family structure. Its leaders advocated a new family system wherein women would be free to choose their own mates, remarry if they wished, and be economically independent. The scope of their critique can be seen in an article in the movement's organ, *New Youth,* which demanded full emancipation of women from household drudgery, proposing that the care of children, preparation of food, laundry, and housecleaning be put on a collective basis. [11]

In 1919 a profound political upsurge shook China. It began with student demonstrations in Peking protesting the concessions of Chinese sovereignty to Japan under the Versailles Treaty at the end of World War I. This movement, called the May Fourth Movement, soon spread to other sectors of the population and evoked a sweeping cultural renovation as well as political radicalism. In the wake of the May Fourth Movement the women's movement reappeared with new vigor.

The traditional family system was widely questioned. Ibsen's plays became particularly popular. Repressive sexual morality was attacked by figures like Hu Shih, Lu Hsun, and other writers who rejected one-sided chastity and the idea that chastity equalled morality.

During 1919 *The New Woman* and *Woman's Bell,* two feminist journals, made their appearance. The first aimed "to rouse women as a means of reforming society," while the second strove to "educate women and en-able them to take part in the progress of society." 12

In the general atmosphere of ferment, women won a number of gains. Coeducation, for example, began to spread. By 1922 twenty-eight universities and colleges had women students. Professional opportunities for educated women increased.

New groups were also organized. In 1920 women in Changsha joined demonstrations demanding marriage freedom and personal freedom. In 1921 the Women's Association of Hunan was established. This group soon became known as the "five proposal movement" after its call for women's right to vote, to be elected to office, to education, to work, and to self-determination in marriage. By December 1921 the Women's Association had succeeded in forcing provisions for women's suffrage and personal freedom into the Hunan constitution and had elected women to the provincial legislature.

Similar movements were organized in Kwantung and Chekiang provinces. In Peking women students organized a Women's Suffrage Association in July 1922. That August a more militant group, the Women's Rights League, was formed. In addition to demanding women's rights, it called upon women to join the revolution to overthrow the warlords and establish democracy.

Several organizations to promote birth control and contraception were also organized in Peking and Shanghai following a visit to China by Margaret Sanger in April 1922.

By the early 1920s the revival of movements struggling for women's rights had progressed to the point that women's organizations existed in virtually every large city and even in a number of peasant communities.

Women played a militant and important role in the growth of the trade-union movement in the early 1920s. For example, in Shanghai in 1923, 20,000 women workers in the silk filatures went on strike to demand a ten-hour workday plus a wage increase of five cents a day.

Two years later 14,000 women again struck the Shanghai silk industry. [13] By 1924 International Women's Day began to be celebrated annually in China. The 1926 strike wave in Shanghai produced an upsurge among women workers. In addition to higher wages and shorter hours, the women demanded medical service, compensation for injuries, and a one-month paid vacation during child birth. [14]

Liu Ch'un-hsien, who later became a leading Communist Party trade unionist, described the conditions in the Kiangsu cotton factory where she worked, conditions not unusual in the textile industry.

Her workday began at 4:30 am, and if workers were even ten minutes late the foreman cursed and threatened them. Many children worked in the factory and they were so tired and sleepy at that hour that, according to Liu, they always cried.

"I used to wonder," she said, "why we had to begin work while the city was asleep, only to get enough to eat. We began working before dawn, and returned after 8 pm. We never saw the sky for months, and some never saw the sun for years. Every day I asked myself, 'When will this hard life stop?' and prayed for the close of the day's work."

The women were paid by piece work, and lived in fear that a machine would break down since that would stop production and cause their wages to suffer. If a machine did break down, the foreman punished the worker by decreasing her wages, in effect forcing the workers to pay for the upkeep of the machinery in the factory.

The foremen had their favorites among the women. "If a girl was beautiful, she was treated better than old women and children, to whom the authorities were terribly cruel. Children were beaten but not the older workers." However, the worst treatment was meted out to attractive women who resisted the advances of the supervisors. Liu lived in a room with nine other women. "Two of them," she recalls, "were old — about thirty-six at least — and married, and they were extremely virtuous, so the foreman treated them very badly."

Her earliest political activity took place in the factory in 1924. A young girl had fallen into a machine and been killed. "Because of this, a group of workers began sabotage for three hours, and forced the authorities to give about thirty dollars to her family. We did not know the political meaning of sabotage; it was purely spontaneous." Later, however, activities were led by workers from Shanghai "who had some political training." 15

In 1970, Chen Pi-lan, a leading member of the Chinese Communist Party in the 1920s and a founder of the Chinese Trotskyist movement, recalled some of the early organizing work done among women workers in Shanghai. Chen was then a leader of the All-Shanghai Women's Federation, which included students, workers, teachers, and intellectuals, and published a monthly magazine called *Chinese Women.*

Chen explained that "our most important work at this time was to organize and educate among the women workers in Shanghai," of whom there were many thousands in the textile and cigarette factories. "We established night schools for discussion and education of women workers. Sometimes we held meetings with them to discuss specific problems of women workers. For instance, a woman worker could only take off about one week to have a baby — and with no pay. Sometimes the women were worked so hard that they had babies right in the factory."

In addition to discussing the specific problems of women workers, the All-Shanghai Women's Federation also explained questions concerning the whole working class. "In this way," she explained, "we helped the women workers to organize unions, especially in factories where all the workers were women, such as the cotton mills, silk factories, and cigarette factories."

Women workers were also organized to take part in street demonstrations under the banners of the All-

Shanghai Women's Federation. These demonstrations sometimes encompassed hundreds of thousands of workers and involved pitched battles with the police and army. On those occasions, "members of the All-Shanghai Women's Federation would come to the front and stand with their banners flying, often displaying more bravery than the men." [16]

The Chinese Communist Party was also organizing peasant women in the 1920s. Chen points out that "when the peasant associations were established by the CCP, the woman question arose immediately. Some women went to the peasant associations and charged their husbands with oppressing them. Others charged their mothers-in-law for the same reason. In some areas of the countryside women's associations were organized to readjust the relationships in the families. For the first time divorces took place in the countryside initiated by the women." [17]

One of the leading early peasant organizations was the Hailufeng Peasant Union formed in 1925. This organization differed from most in that it included both men's and women's unions. About one-fourth of the seven thousand members of the joint union were women. In Hailufeng there was also a General Women's Union made up of peasants, students, teachers, and industrial workers, with over one thousand members. Ts'ai Ting-li, a woman leader in Hailufeng, described the impact of the General Women's Union:

"All were young, and they were enthusiastic about their recent release from suppression. Some of the men hated this organization because it defended the rights of women and took care of the divorce problem. A woman could come to the union to complain against her husband's or family's treatment, and the union would investigate the case and see to it that the woman either received better treatment or was given a divorce. It was teasingly called the 'Bureau for Divorce and Remarriage.'"

Concubines, who were often the real wives in China

but had no legal rights or protection, were prominent in the leadership of the union. The membership was very youthful, with the oldest members being under thirty and the youngest twelve and thirteen.

Ts'ai recalled that "in the early period women did not do any of the fighting, but in fighting pirates and bandits they did transportation work in the rear. Many times the bandits scattered when they had been defeated, and the women and children acted as spies and caught them."

The prime movers in the women's work in Hailufeng were female industrial workers, and women usually took the leadership in the trade unions there, although the real direction came from the Communist Party. 18

The changing role of women found its reflection in the laws as well. By 1915 the courts had begun to accept that there should be freedom of marriage and that family members could own property separately.

The decline into warlordism after 1915 proved not to be a simple repetition of previous precapitalist collapses of a dynastic government. The new warlord chieftains sought the protection of foreign imperialist powers and, while selling their country's economy to the highest bidder, sought to emulate the legal and cultural forms of their imperialist patrons. After the defeat of the workers' revolution of 1925-27 at the hands of the rising bourgeois party of Chiang Kai-shek, the Kuomintang (KMT), the country was unified under the KMT, which paid lip service to Western-style reforms. Studies showed that by the 1930s the majority of educated youth in Kuomintang China had come to believe in marriage based on free choice. 19

The 1931 Kuomintang civil code adopted the principle of freedom of marriage and the equality of women. Divorce was now legal, although on restricted grounds that did not include objections to the husband taking concubines. Many of these legal changes remained solely on paper. In general it was only in the urban areas that women's position was altered, and even there the adherence to the new standards was very uneven.

China remained a vast agricultural nation. Land reform was needed both to bring China into the industrial age and to break down the patriarchal village clan system that imprisoned peasant women. In Western Europe the rising capitalist class had to extend the right of bourgeois property to the land in order to bring the land under the control of the industrial bourgeoisie. In the underdeveloped countries, however, imperialism usually takes the precapitalist modes of production as it finds them and converts them to production for the world market without reforming them. In China the new bourgeoisie was tied to the landlord system not only because of the interests of foreign imperialism. In imperial times the mandarin ruling bureaucracy, unlike the rural feudal lords of Europe, lived in the cities. Thus the bourgeoisie grew up under the thumb of the old ruling class and even drew its membership from mandarins who went into business. Thus there were close family ties between the bourgeoisie, the imperial bureaucracy, and the landlords. As Harold Isaacs put it, the Chinese bourgeoisie "was bound by a thousand links to the precapitalist or semi-feudal system of exploitation of the land."[20] As a result, even the limited rights won by women in the course of the bourgeois revolutions against feudalism in Europe were not fully realizable under the bourgeois Kuomintang but would have to be ushered in by a socialist revolution against both capitalism and the precapitalist relations on the land.

THE COMMUNIST PARTY AND THE WOMEN'S MOVEMENT BEFORE 1949

The history of the Chinese Communist Party's relations with the struggle for women's emancipation must be divided into two distinct parts: the period prior to 1927, when it saw the women's movement as an ally on the road to a socialist revolution; and the period afterward when, while championing the fight against the worst abuses of the precapitalist past, the party under Stalinist leadership increasingly viewed the women's movement as subordinate to the party and often sought to limit the demands of women to enforcement of the democratic provisions of the KMT law code rather than going beyond them to full emancipation.

The early years of the Chinese CP were tremendously influenced by the example of the Russian Revolution and the revolutionary program of the Bolshevik Party. Between 1917 and 1927 the Soviet government passed a whole series of laws giving women formal legal equality with men, revamping marriage and divorce laws, and granting free abortions on demand as every woman's right. The 1919 program of the Soviet CP stated that "the party's task at the present moment is primarily work in the realm of ideas and education so as to destroy utterly all traces of the former inequality or prejudices, particularly among backward strata of the proletariat and peasantry. Not confining itself to formal equality of women, the party strives to liberate them from the material burdens of obsolete household work by replacing it by communal houses, public eating places, central laundries, nurseries, etc."

Under this influence, the CCP was characterized by an unstinting commitment to the women's movement. The manifesto of the Second Congress of the CCP in July 1922 called for the right to vote for all, regardless of sex, and for the abolition of all legislation restricting women. During the 1920s the CCP was instrumental in calling a large number of representative conferences to organize peasant and working women. It formed the leadership of the militant National Women's Association, which had 300,000 members during the 1925-27 period. [21]

The fate of the women's movement was inextricably linked with that of the overall revolutionary movement. In the early 1920s the CCP experienced a tremendous growth. From a small handful it was transformed into a mass party with influence among millions of workers and peasants. The great revolutionary upsurge that opened in 1925 went down to defeat, however, as a result of policies imposed on the young Communist Party by the Stalinist leadership of the Communist International.

From its inception, the Comintern had urged that Communist parties in the colonial and semicolonial countries support any independence struggles against imperialism, even if led by bourgeois-nationalist forces. But it insisted that Communist parties in these areas, while supporting the national liberation struggles, must maintain their organizational independence from the bourgeois forces and must retain their freedom to advance demands in the interests of the workers as opposed to the bourgeois forces.

With this stipulation it was permissible in China to aspire to a united front of the Kuomintang and the CCP against the imperialist powers and native warlords. In August 1922, however, the Comintern's representative in China, Dutch CPer Henryk Sneevliet (using the pseudonym Maring), reinterpreted the "united front" tactic to include membership of CCPers in the Kuomintang. Sneevliet called a plenum of the CCP's central committee and, against the strenuous objections of the Chinese CP leaders, insisted that CCP members join the Kuomintang as a bloc.

A January 12, 1923, resolution of the Executive Committee of the Communist International stressed, however, that while "supporting the Kuomintang in all campaigns on the national-revolutionary front, so long as it follows an objectively correct policy, the Chinese Communist Party nevertheless must not fuse with it and during these campaigns must not furl its own flag."[22]

When Stalin came to the helm in the Soviet CP, Sneevliet's mistaken policy was compounded. The Kuomintang was made a "sympathizing section" of the Communist International, and was the recipient of massive Soviet aid, which transformed it from a loose federation of tendencies into a tightly disciplined bourgeois party with its own army.

Stalin had justified this policy of subordination of the CCP to the Kuomintang by advancing the theory that a socialist revolution would have to be made in two stages. First, the Communist Party would have to join hands with the capitalists to drive out foreign imperialism, defeat the warlords, and unify the country. Then, after a prolonged period — many decades — of capitalist development, the working class would proceed to the socialist revolution. But the bourgeoisie, owing to its links with the landholding classes and with foreign capital, was incapable of playing a progressive role, of accomplishing the traditional tasks of the bourgeois revolution. By its policy of restraining the masses in order to maintain its alliance with the so-called progressive bourgeoisie, the CCP effectively disarmed the masses, paving the way for the 1927 massacre of the Shangai workers.

In 1925 the Kuomintang, with CCP support, had seized power around Canton and set up an antiwarlord government. In March of 1926 Chiang Kai-shek established his dictatorial rule over the Canton regime, and in April 1927 Chiang, in the course of his Northern Expedition to defeat the provincial warlords, used his troops to brutally crush a successful workers' uprising in Shanghai. Tens of thousands of the most radical workers and women activists were killed, marking the beginning of the end of the period of revolutionary upsurge.

In the 1927 purge, Chiang Kai-shek was particularly vindictive against women activists, destroying most of the women's associations. Stalin, as a futile gesture of resistance after his policies had led to defeat in the main revolutionary centers, ordered an uprising in Canton in December 1927. When this was suppressed some two or three hundred women were executed by the Kuomintang for simply being caught with short haircuts, a symbol of emancipation.[23] More than 1,000 women leaders were killed during this bloody year of reaction.[24]

The year 1927 also saw the culmination of a process of bureaucratization of the Chinese Communist Party. Until then it had carried out Stalin's policies reluctantly and only under protest. After the Shanghai massacre the party's founder and general secretary Ch'en Tu-hsiu was made a scapegoat for the failure and removed from his post. Henceforth leaders of the CCP were chosen for their agreement with Stalin's line.

Following the defeat, sections of the CCP retreated to the countryside, establishing a peasant army and "red bases" in Hunan and Kiangsi. This was part of a worldwide period of ultraleftism in the Comintern. This ultraleftism, which in the Stalinist schema came to be known as the "third period," was prompted by a number of factors. First among these was the internal crisis of the Soviet Union. Stalin's faction of the Soviet CP had resisted rapid industrialization and had instead relied on a policy of allowing the rich peasants to increase their wealth, despite the Trotskyist prediction that such a policy would lead to an eventual attempt by the rich peasants to destroy the Soviet power. When this in fact happened, with the peasants withholding grain from the cities, the Stalinists were forced to turn on the rich peasants and institute forced collectivization. In order to outflank the Trotskyists and other independent revolutionists to the left, who had predicted that Stalin's past policy would be disastrous, the Stalinists adopted a wildly ultraleft policy throughout the world.

This period in Comintern politics lasted until 1935, when a turn to collaboration with bourgeois parties in "popular fronts" was decided on.

In the rural base areas that the CP retreated to, the status of women changed dramatically under the impact of mass mobilizations. They were granted inheritance and property rights as well as freedom of marriage and divorce. Ten thousand women in the Kiangsi base area participated in local unions. Women were also organized into brigades to make clothing and shoes for the Red Army. They were mobilized to work in the fields while the men fought at the front, and in many villages women were organized into guerrilla groups to defend the area when the men were absent.[25]

In *Fanshen,* William Hinton gives a vivid illustration of the change that took place in the lives of peasant women in the areas controlled by the CCP. Hsein-e, a peasant woman, requested a divorce from her husband who had nearly beaten her to death. Never before had there been a divorce in her village. To win the support of the villagers Hsein-e appeared before a mass meeting and recounted the sufferings she had endured. Through this emotional experience, the masses were convinced and voted overwhelmingly in favor of her being granted a divorce.[26]

Land reform, property rights, and the right to divorce gave women a new independence and dignity that are expressed in these few simple statements by peasant women:

"When I get my share I'll separate from my husband. Then he won't oppress me any more."

"Always before when we quarrelled my husband said 'get out of my house.' Now I can give it right back to him. I can say 'get out of my house, yourself.'"[27]

The rural base areas in Kiangsi, however, were unable to sustain the CCP against the Chiang regime's attacks. Therefore on October 18, 1934, the base was abandoned and the Chinese Red Army began what has become known as the "Long March" into Northeast China.

Before it arrived in northern Shensi province 366 days later, the Red Army would cover more than six thousand miles on foot under almost constant attack by Chiang's armies. 100,000 soldiers left Kiangsi and approximately 25,000 more were recruited along the way. But in the first ten weeks alone nearly 60,000 men and officers were killed or wounded. By the time the march ended, less than 20,000 troops remained in the army.

Only fifty women participated in the Long March, and they were restricted to special roles within the army — particularly the public health and supply corps. One woman, Ku'o Chun-Ch'ing, disguised herself as a man, rose rapidly through the ranks, and was awarded the army's highest award — "distinguished serviceman." However, it was discovered that she was a woman when she was wounded and taken to a hospital. Upon her recovery she was reassigned to the public health section with the other women.[28]

It was in January 1935, in the course of the Long March, that Mao Tse-Tung emerged as the central leader of the CCP, a preeminence that was secured in 1945 by a purge of his remaining opponents in the party hierarchy.

The CCP's arrival at Yenan in northern Shensi province coincided with the Communist International's right turn toward Popular Frontism. The Chinese Stalinists then sought to renew the collaboration with Chiang Kaishek that had been broken by Chiang's massacre in 1927.

Japan, which had already taken large sections of Manchuria and northern China, was clearly planning a further invasion. In December 1936 some of Chiang's officers at Sian captured the generalissimo and were prepared to execute him if he wouldn't sanction a common front with the CCP against the impending invasion. Stalin personally called on the CCP to intervene to save Chiang's life, and Chou En-lai went to Sian where he negotiated a new agreement with Chiang for Kuomintang-CCP cooperation.

As its part of the bargain, the CCP dropped its program for land reform, agreed to recognize Chiang as the Supreme Commander of all anti-Japanese military forces, and downplayed the activities of the women's organizations. It stressed that the main role of the women's movement during the war with Japan was to organize women for productive activity. Changing its position toward marriage, it no longer referred to the "abolition of the feudal family." During this period, which lasted almost ten years from 1936 to 1945, the CCP backtracked on the principle of freedom of divorce, which it had advocated during the Kiangsi period, introducing a series of restrictions on this right.

Women did play an important part in the resistance against the Japanese invaders. They took part, for example , in the 1935 demonstrations against the Japanese in Peiping (later Peking). In December 1935 the Women's National Salvation Association was formed in Shanghai and organized demonstrations around slogans such as "Stop Civil War," "Form a United Front Against Japan to Save the Nation," and "Women Can Emancipate Themselves Only Through Participation in the Resistance." Women's magazines also appeared, among them *Women's Life, Women Masses,* and *Little Sister.* The Shanghai and Tsingtao textile workers, who were mostly female, walked out in tens of thousands from Japanese owned cotton mills. [29]

At the end of the war, the CCP opened negotiations

with Chiang for admission into the Kuomintang government as a minority party. Its professed aim was to build
a "New Democratic" China in cooperation with the Kuomintang. It limited its program, including on women's
issues, to those acceptable in principle to the liberals in
the KMT. Chiang rejected the urgings of his American
advisors to accept Mao's offer and instead launched a
military attack in July 1946 on the territories the Maoists had taken from the Japanese. The Maoists resisted
and, after some hesitations, adopted a more radical
social program to spur mass mobilizations that were
needed to win the fight against Chiang. This included
more radical positions on the family and divorce. Women
were encouraged to struggle against the "feudal" family.
CCP women's groups organized "Speak Bitterness" sessions where groups of women would gather in the villages and publicly recount the humiliations of the old
system, the beatings, the rapes. This unique form of
struggle served to translate the personal anguish of
women into a collective anger against the system.

Women took action against their oppressive masters.
First the offending males were warned politely; if they
then didn't comply, they found themselves subject to
the fury of the women's association. Jack Belden in his
China Shakes the World describes such a scene:

"The crowd fell on him, howling, knocked him to the
ground, then jumped on him with their feet. . . . Those
in the rear leaped in, tore at his clothing, then seized
his bare flesh in their hands and began twisting and
squeezing till his blood flowed from many scratches. . . .
Chang let out an anguished howl. 'Don't beat me! Don't
beat me,' he bleated in terror. 'I'll reform. Don't hurt
me any more.' Under the blows of the women, his cries
were soon stilled. The women backed off. Gold Flower
peered down at her husband. He lay there motionless
on the ground, like a dead dog, his mouth full of mud,
his clothes in tatters and blood coming in a slow trickle

from his nose. 'That's how it was with me in the past,' Gold Flower thought. Unable to restrain a feeling of happiness, she turned to the other women. 'Many thanks, comrade sisters, for your kindness. If it had not been for you, I would not have been able to get my revenge.'" 30

THE POLICY TOWARD WOMEN
AFTER THE REVOLUTION

The Chinese civil war ended in October 1949 with a Maoist victory over Chiang's Kuomintang and the proclamation of the People's Republic of China in Peking. Mao and his associates stood at the head of a vast mass movement that they sought to channel into the building of a "New Democratic" China much on the lines of the proposals the CCP had made to Chiang at the end of World War II. This indefinitely deferred socialist measures such as nationalization of industry or communal facilities that could relieve women's economic burdens in the family. Nevertheless, the upsurge of the masses led to profound and deep-going reforms of the old system.

The China Democratic Women's Federation was set up at this time with the dual responsibility of implementing government policy toward women and of bringing to the government's attention complaints by women when the approved reforms were not being implemented. In 1949 the federation had 20 million members and was to grow to 76 million by 1956. [31]

Women were given the right to vote. Prostitution and female infanticide were prohibited, and to a large extent abolished in practice. [32] The new marriage laws gave women their rights to property, inheritance, and free choice in marriage, divorce, and custody of children. [33]

Concubinage was forbidden, although no action was taken on this unless one of the women involved complained. [34] The Chinese government reported that with the beginning of land reform, 60 million women acquired land equality with men in central and eastern China alone. [35]

Chinese women regarded the overthrow of the Chiang Kai-shek dictatorship as a fundamental turning point after which their rights would be granted. The CCP sought to consolidate its new power by energetically attempting to uproot the potentially hostile structures of the village clan elders and the patriarchal family system. To this end it encouraged women to attack some of the worst features of the traditional family and to organize against their oppression. However, the CCP placed limits on this drive, for while encouraging attacks against the traditional family and social structures, it did not go as far as to promote the Bolshevik program for the emancipation of women.

In 1950 a new Marriage Law was passed in China. According to Teng Ying-Chao, vice president of the All-China Democratic Women's Federation, the purpose of the law was "to ensure to people the full freedom of marriage, and to deal a death blow to the old marriage system." [36]

Article 1 of the new law stated that "the arbitrary and compulsory feudal marriage system, which is based on the superiority of man over woman and which ignores the children's interests shall be abolished." The new law, the article continued, is based on "free choice of partners, on monogamy, on equal rights for both sexes, and on protection of the lawful interests of women and children."

Another article stated that "bigamy, concubinage, child betrothal, interference with the re-marriage of widows and the exaction of money or gifts in connection with marriage shall be prohibited."

The articles dealing with divorce established a system wherein divorce was a simple matter of registration of the proper papers when both parties agreed to divorce, and in cases where only one party desired it, the case would be mediated and settled by a people's court.

Response to the law was immediate. Women particularly took advantage of the divorce provisions. In Shanghai, for example, nearly 91 percent of the divorces cases in 1950 were initiated by women. [37] Between 78 and 82 percent of the divorce actions in that year were based on "the arbitrary and compulsory marriage system, the buying and selling of wives, ill-treatment of women-folk, child marriage, bigamy, adultery, and desertion." [38]

From 1950 to 1953 the CCP launched a mass campaign to enforce the new marriage laws. Propaganda exhibitions, leaflets, pictorial handbooks understandable to the mass of illiterate people, and plays conveyed the message to the countryside. Stories in the press dwelt continuously on the theme of progressive children versus their backward parents. Some 3.5 million CCP cadres were given training courses in the new laws. In Honan province, of the 240 theater groups set up in 1952, 25 percent of the plays performed centered around the marriage laws and how to deal with family conflicts. [39]

Women met deep resistance to their fight for equality from the peasant males. Old traditions clung tenaciously and the laws were often opposed or subverted by backward husbands, including party cadres. Males often resented the undermining of their authority in both the family and the village community. Divorce might run against their economic interests, for through it they lost a wife who provided domestic labor and her property as well. Some older women felt threatened by the freedom of choice in marriage, as it undermined their control over their daughters and daughter-in-law, the one small share of power they were familiar with in the old society.

One charge frequently leveled against the new Marriage Law, according to Teng Ying-Shao, vice president of the All-China Democratic Women's Federation, was that "the Law 'leans to the women's side.'"

She pointed out that in some rural areas, resistance to the new concepts of women's equality in marriage was so strong that "there are still found many cases of women being killed, or committing suicide as a result of the absence of the freedom of divorce."[40] According to Chou En-lai more than ten thousand women committed suicide because of "the oppression of families" in the first half of 1951 alone.[41]

There were cases where female activists who were sent to villages to introduce the new law were murdered by peasant men. Some women were killed by their fathers for defying traditional customs. This pressure was exacerbated by the fact that many male Communist Party cadres, who were now the main political power at the local level, refused to implement the marriage laws. As one reporter put it, these men "because of their alignments with the vested male interests on the village level, used their new authority to actually oppose women's progressive demands."[42]

The CCP hierarchy, anxious to use the new marriage law as a bludgeon against the traditional social structures that might threaten its rule, ran up against the fact that its cadres, whom the party had never trained in the Marxist concept of the liberation of women, were anxious to maintain their male position of superiority in family and social matters and therefore resisted the application of the new law.

The problem of male party cadres opposing the new status of women was highlighted in a report on the new marriage law by Teng Ying-chao, who pointed out that "to guarantee the correct carrying out of the Marriage Law the cadres should first abide by the Law themselves." This, she asserted, was not taking place. "Some of the cadres . . . even dictate other people's matrimonial arrangements, preventing women of their villages from marrying men from other villages or forcing people to marry or divorce. Such phenomena must be strictly corrected," she said. "Every member of the

Communist Party must abide by and carry out the Law faithfully." If cadres continued to refuse, she warned, they would suffer legal and party consequences. [43]

The Department of the Interior of the People's Republic of China reported in October 1951, about a year and a half after the promulgation of the marriage law: "A very common phenomenon is . . . the adopting of antagonistic attitudes toward the Marriage Law by some subdistrict and village cadres. . . . Some even use imprisonment and torturing to handle marriage cases [in an effort to enforce the traditional marriage against women opponents]." [44]

Liu Chang-fan, vice-president of the National Commission on the Marriage Law, reported that the propaganda campaign of March and April 1953 had been largely successful in only 15 percent of the country and completely unsuccessful in 25 percent. A report from Shensi province showed that 90 percent of the marriages had been arranged by parents, although in certain areas as high as 88 percent were based on free choice. The selling of women was still going on under various guises; cash transactions being made secretly. [45]

Changes in the traditional patterns came more rapidly in the cities, where these ideas had already percolated for a longer time. A survey of eleven large and medium cities showed that close to 97.6 percent of the marriages in the first part of 1954 were based on free choice. [46]

The first big campaigns, pushed forward by women activists, made significant inroads on the old patriarchal family. This was a dramatic improvement in the status of women and won a wide measure of popularity for the regime among women. The tempestuous change of the first years after liberation was not maintained, however.

During the first years the CCP had attempted to reconcile its rule with the continuation of a capitalist economy under the program of "New Democracy," which included establishing bourgeois democratic rights for women. But during the Korean war the rich peasants, the Kuomintang holdovers in the civil service bureaucracy, and the thousands of small-factory owners provided a seedbed for sabotaging the economy and raising an opposition to the government of the People's Republic.

The CCP hierarchy decided, therefore, to scrap the "New Democracy" program. In 1953, the first five-year plan was put into effect, marking the break with capitalism and the creation of the planned economy of a workers' state. Having consolidated its power and broken the hold of the precapitalist village structures, the CCP sought stability and saw a militant women's movement as disruptive of this goal. Therefore the CCP ordered a retrenchment in the women's movement.

The new line adopted in 1953 was that women's liberation was completed and no longer required independent struggles by women. This position was summed up by an article entitled "How Should Family Women Better Serve Socialist Reconstruction," in the October 1955 issue of the Peking magazine *Hsin Chung-kuo fu-nü* (*New China's Women*):

"The new Constitution has guaranteed women's equality with men in political, economic, cultural, social, and family interests, and the state has come to protect women's rights in marriage, in the family, in motherhood, and in the welfare of children. Henceforth, women no longer need to initiate a militant struggle for such things."/47/

Women's political role was downplayed and an increasing emphasis was placed on mobilizing women for economic production, combined with appeals to women to perform their family duties well. The struggle for production quotas became primary over the struggle for the realization of feminist demands. This led to a certain reassertion of traditional patterns in the rural areas. In 1955 the Democratic Women's League in a rural coastal town reported great difficulty in distributing 400 copies of the marriage-law books. The CCP's own mass organizations would not accept them, in contrast to 1953.[48] A report from Shensi by a correspondent of an official CCP newspaper revealed that after 1953 the Women's Association, the Youth League, and the People's Councils had not bothered about the marriage laws except in homicide cases. It noted a revival of arranged marriages, and that those who tried to resist them usually lost courage for lack of support from the local officials.[49]

After 1953, divorce became extremely difficult to obtain, family mediation being stressed. While the CCP opposed arranged marriages under the control of the old system of clan elders or parents, it insisted on obtaining party approval before members of the party could marry. Also, with its concept of party discipline extending to every member of society, it is common for the party to use considerations such as local need for particular skills, "bad" family background of individuals, or a record of political opposition as grounds for justifying long-term involuntary separations of married couples even if they are not party members. One observer summed up the new trend in 1957:

"Party propaganda today is heavily weighed with dedication to family unity, discipline and loyalty. Children who neglect their elderly parents are brought to court and punished. Stress is continually laid on filial devotion."[50]

With the Great Leap Forward in the fall of 1958 there was a certain reversal of the attitudes toward divorce and the family. The communes sought to mobilize the entire population under party control for a vast increase in productivity. To draw women into the workforce more fully, important efforts were made to free them from household drudgery. As part of this program, the rural communes set up collective kitchens, child-care centers, and laundries. These progressive steps could not be successfully maintained, however, because of the inadequate resources devoted to them. When the peasant commune members discovered that the food was better at home than in the commune kitchen, they began to stop coming to the kitchens and these ultimately had to be abandoned.

The reasons for the failure of the Great Leap Forward were not directly connected to its reforms in the area of family life. Rather, the attempt to reorganize several traditional villages under a single commune administration, dominated by party officials, was met with hostility by the peasants. This was intensified when it became clear that the new party centralism in the rural areas went hand-in-hand with a drastic lengthening in the workday and a decline in the real standard of living as the state took from the peasants a larger share of the harvest to provision the cities and for industrial uses.

Thus the overall impact of the Great Leap was negative, although it appears that particular measures such as the child-care arrangements and laundry facilities were in themselves popular. The peasants and workers reacted to the enforced mobilization by what amounted to a massive sit-down strike. One historian reports:

"The per capita output of food crops, taking 1957 as 100, fell from the 112 attained in 1958 to 88 in 1959 and to 81 in 1960. . . . In December 1960 the PRC began buying wheat on the world market. . . . Industrial output tumbled by approximately 75 percent in 1961 as compared with the peak output attained by the Great Leap Forward in 1959-60." 51

The revelations of the Cultural Revolution of the late 1960s show that Mao Tse-tung, who had engineered the program of bureaucratic speedup and mobilization of the Great Leap period, was removed from effective exercise of power at the Central Committee plenum held at Lushan in August 1959. He was replaced as head of state by Liu Shao-ch'i, who reverted to the previous pattern of administration, relying on material incentives and social conservatism to increase production rather than political indoctrination and party discipline as Mao had done. The result of Liu's policies was an increase in the standard of living and a relaxation of the military-style party control over daily life, but it also involved a strengthening of the hold of the family as a stabilizing influence.

Ai-li S. Chin, in her survey of Chinese periodicals from 1960 to 1966, noted the stress on authority and dedication rather than rebellion and independence. The Chinese woman, she said, is glorified for being capable and progressive, yet praised for being "demure" and "self-effacing." [52]

When Jan Myrdal, a Swedish journalist sympathetic to Maoism, questioned some villagers in 1962 on the question of divorce he was told:

"But that [divorce] is a thing of the past. If there are children, people think it is immoral and wicked to leave them. Even if the marriage is childless, people still consider divorce immoral, because now people can choose whom they will marry, they will have chosen each other and should put up with the consequences. One can always adopt a child. If in spite of all this, they still want a divorce the various organizations, the party, the League of Youth, the women's group, try to instruct them and explain what is the decent thing to do and the one consistent with socialist moralists. If they persist, the matter is taken up by the mediation committee of the people's commune which goes into it thoroughly with them and explains to them why they ought not divorce but live together and agree. If after all this they refuse to give in and still want a divorce, they are of course entitled to go to the court in Yenan and start proceedings for divorce but that has not happened in Liu Ling, nor have any divorces been heard of in many years for it is a long time now since women were granted equality and marriages have been entered into equally."[53]

Recent visitors to China report that a similar attitude towards divorce prevails today. This overwhelming social pressure against divorce hits women more severely than men because many women are caught in oppressive relationships with husbands who are still steeped in the patriarchal tradition. The Cultural Revolution, with its upheaval within the bureaucracy, brought some renewed criticism of the continuing patriarchal structure of the family. But its only lasting impact appears to have been in an improvement of women's pay scales in relation to men. The organized opposition to divorce remains.

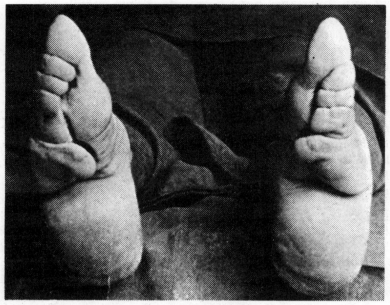

Above: The ideal "Golden Lotus" bound foot, shown here at actual size, three inches from heel to toe.
Below: Children in Kindergarten No. 1 in Sian.

Above: Nurses with Maoist Eighth Route Army in 1938. Right: "Barefoot Doctors" in countryside.

Above: Commune women collecting the harvest.
Below: Hofei Polytechnical Institute students in school factory.

Militia women training.

WOMEN AND EDUCATION

Equal education, while not necessarily guaranteeing equality in other spheres, certainly is a very important prerequisite for Chinese women's advancement in the political and economic life of the country. The CCP was faced with a massive problem of illiteracy, particularly among women. A sample survey in the nine counties of Szechuan province in South China in 1942 and 1943 showed 48 percent of the men to be literate, but only 19 percent of the women.[54] After 1949, mass literacy campaigns were launched to combat this problem. In 1950 in the Shanghai textile factories, where a majority of the employees are women, 170 literacy groups were organized with a total membership of 9,000. In the cities of Darien and Port Arthur, out of 9,115 illiterate women workers in 1951, some 94.5 percent participated in literacy programs.[55] In 1958 more than 16 million women passed their literacy tests.[56] I have found no recent figures on the extent of present illiteracy. Undoubtedly it remains a problem, but it is clear that a significant effort has been made with impressive results.

Little sex-role differentiation exists at the primary and lower levels of education. The schools train "both sexes to enter the same job market; this counters the informal socialization process at home and in the community which trains boys and girls for different jobs." [57]

The proportion of women in schools increased from 25 percent in 1949 to 30 percent in 1958 at the primary level, from 20 to 31 percent at the technical middle-school level, and from 18 percent to 23 percent in the institutions of higher learning. [58] Over nine years time and after a socialist revolution, however, the increases, which range from 5 percent to 11 percent, are not dramatic. Schooling as a whole, particularly college level, was drastically curtailed during both the Great Leap Forward and again during the Cultural Revolution, the two high tides of distinctly Maoist policy. The results, while not aimed at women especially, were to greatly reduce educational opportunities for all Chinese youth. Ross Terrill, the Australian China scholar and Labor Party spokesman, visited China in the summer of 1971. He reported:

"After two or three years without classes, many universities began again last fall with a small, handpicked enrollment. At Peking University . . . where there used to be 9,000 students, the new class of September, 1970, numbered 2,667. . . . An astonishing number of the new students are members of the Party or the Communist Youth League. At S.Y.S.U. [Sun Yat-sen University in Canton], for instance, 229 of the 547 students are Chinese Communist party and another 240 are CYL members." [59]

While general figures on the percentage of women students among the reduced student bodies of the institutions of higher education are lacking, partial evidence would lead one to believe that it is no higher than before the Cultural Revolution. The Committee of Concerned Asian Scholars was told in 1971 during their trip to China that women comprised 30 percent of the student body at Peking University. [60] And using Terrill's figures on the percentage of Communist Party and Communist Youth League members at S. Y. S. U. as an indicator, we can assume that women are underrepresented at that school as well, since female membership in the CCP has always been drastically below the proportion of women in the population.

Even today, the traditional family roles women are expected to play begin early to eliminate them from the road to higher education. Thus Linda Gordon, who teaches women's history at the University of Massachusetts, visited China in December 1972 and reported of one production brigade at the Red Mountain Commune:

"We visited the primary school, which is compulsory, and it had 50 percent girl students; the junior middle school, which is not compulsory, had only 20 percent girl students. When we asked why, the chairman of the revolutionary committee of the brigade said there were many more boys than girls born in that region. . . . We asked him again, this time in a large formal discussion with many people from the brigade. When he said the same thing, the chairwoman of our delegation said flatly that we did not believe it. There was a long silence after the translator had communicated that remark. Finally, a woman sitting in the back of the room said that she thought the reason there were so few girls in the junior middle school was that the girls were expected to do the housework."[61]

It would, of course, be completely wrong to expect that China could rapidly carry out measures that require an industrially advanced economy. But that is no excuse for a retreat on measures that can be introduced now. Equally wrong is the tendency among radical Western visitors to leave their critical faculties behind when they visit China simply because the revolution has led to advances in many areas. This is an example of liberal adaptation to the regime, the same kind that led many Western socialists and liberals to uphold the Stalin dictatorship against the Russian working class and Russian women in the 1930s and 1940s.

The Maoist regime, the Chinese variety of Stalinism, has presided over many profound and important gains

for women secured by the planned economy instituted in 1953. But the CCP's conscious policy has often been aimed at subordinating women's demands to
considerations of party discipline, placation of backward tendencies, privileges for the administrative hierarchy, and an undisguised sympathy of the regime for
the bourgeois family while opposing the horrors of precapitalist oppression of women.

WOMEN AND THE WORK FORCE

To support its claim that Chinese women are emancipated, the CCP points to and stresses the accomplishments made in integrating women into the productive life of the nation. Real gains have been made in this area, but they are more uneven than the Maoist press generally suggests. There has been no steady climb in the number of working women; rather, the number has varied according to the rate of economic growth, the priorities of the various sectors of the economy, and the shifting economic policies between the Maoist and Liuist factions in the leadership.

When the regime is seeking a rapid increase in productivity through a mobilization of labor power, it praises the liberating effects of being a working woman. When it cannot absorb women into production, however, it glorifies the home.

The existing statistics on women workers in China are scanty and can be misleading. For example, between 1949 and 1957 the number of women employed by industry rose from 500,000 to 3 million. [62] In the same period, however, the overall population grew by some 2 percent a year and the spread of industrialization added male as well as female workers to the labor force.

As a proportion of the total number of workers in industry, the real increase for women was only 2 percentage points, from 15 percent in 1949 to 17 percent in 1957.

Before 1949 there was a relatively high concentration of women working in the light industries, such as textiles. Under the CCP regime they began to enter new areas of work. In the cities of Darien and Port Arthur in 1951, for instance, there were 1,196 women in 35 kinds of technical and skilled jobs in heavy industry, including operating lathes, repairing ships, and metal casting.[63] Women professors, lecturers, and assistant professors soared from 2,319 in 1949 to 11,207 in 1957.[64] The proportion of women in medicine and engineering is much higher in China than in the advanced capitalist nations. In 1960, 42 percent of the medical students and 17 percent of the engineering students were women.[65]

The Chinese press abounds with stories of women entering traditionally male enclaves. Women operate heavy construction equipment, drive trucks, wield picks on roadgangs, drive locomotives, and serve in the militia. In 1956 women constituted 25 percent of Chinese railway workers. and in 1957 China had a squadron of jet fighters run entirely by women.[66]

In agriculture it is hard to estimate the actual increase in labor done by women, because of the lack of statistics. A survey by John Lossing Buck for the period 1929-33 showed that women made up only 25.36 percent of the rural labor force engaged in farm and subsidiary work (this did not include housework, which is why the figure is so low).[67] By 1955 women accounted for 45.2 percent of the employed in the cooperative farms, and in 1957, while this figure had dropped to 43.3 percent, the number of peasants in cooperatives had grown drastically.[68]

The integration of women into the workforce is crucial to their gaining economic independence, increasing their status, and broadening their range of choices. But the liberating effect of productive work can be sharply under-cut if not accompanied by adequate daycare and communal facilities, relieving women of their domestic duties. One need only look at the capitalist states, where working women continue to be weighed down by the full burden of household chores and childcare.

In this realm China had made incomparably more progress than under capitalism. Still this is clearly not a top priority of the CCP regime, and the lack of such facilities continues to be a major barrier to the equal participation of women in the labor force. The impressive percentage of women employees in the cooperatives, for example, does not reflect the fewer number of days women work because of their household responsibilities, nor the lower pay they receive for their labor.

After the revolution, an auspicious beginning was made in organizing childcare facilities. By 1951, the number of nurseries in the cities had increased ninefold since the CCP took power, with more than 15,700 nurseries, kindergartens, and other types of childcare centers providing for some 520,000 children. For agricultural workers there were seasonal nursery units that looked after 800,000 children during the busy farming periods. But there are roughly 100 million young children in China. Thus this catered to less than 2 percent of the needs, not taking into account that most of the day-care was only of a temporary nature. 69

This posed a serious objective problem that the regime would have to surmount not only to achieve the emancipation of women, but to make available women's productive power for economic growth. The scope of the needs that still had to be tackled in 1951 can be gauged in this description by Hsü Chuan in a letter to the editor that appeared in the March 8, 1952, issue of the Peking *Jen-min jih-pao*:

"In Peking there were only eleven nurseries before the Liberation, and these have increased to sixty-five [February 1951], fifty-seven of which have been attached to public offices. Recently four nursing rooms have been added. But in Peking there are over four hundred government offices, over eight hundred schools, and over thirty comparatively large factories. Because of the absence of nurseries and nursing rooms in the vast majority of the government offices, women cadres cannot work with ease of mind, and some of them have even stopped working. Some unmarried women comrades, seeing the burden of motherhood, are unwilling to get married, and those already married resort to contraception."[70]

But in the years of rapid economic growth that followed, day-care facilities in the urban areas actually decreased. *Jen-min jih-pao* reported on August 5, 1955, that only 165,000 children were under care in the urban areas, as compared to the 1951 figure of 520,000.[71] In part the decrease seems to have been caused by an industrial slump in 1954, although even the official press over the next few years noted a tendency of CCP administrators to discriminate against women in a large variety of jobs, despite their adequate qualifications. As there was no labor shortage, the officials found it too troublesome to employ women because nurseries would then have to be set up and maternity leave with pay provided.[72]

At the Eighth Party Congress in September 1956, Ts'ai Ch'ang, a member of the CP central committee since 1928 and head of the All-China Democratic Women's Congress (renamed the National Women's Federation in 1957), delivered a speech on the role of women in which she objected to these commonly held attitudes. She was seconded by Yang Chih-hua, who attacked the attitude that regarded employment of women as "uneconomical and presenting too many problems."[73]

This backtracking on the employment of women was reflected on the ideological level in 1956 in the "Five Good Program," which was an attempt to restore the glories of the home. Instead of being urged to participate in the work force, or even being told simply that for the moment jobs were not available, women were told to arrange their homes in proper order, to help and unite with neighbors, to encourage their husbands to work and study well, to educate their children in the proper way, and to study hard themselves.

The Third Congress of the All-China Democratic Women's Federation in September 1957 advised women that "to diligently and thriftily manage the home" was as much a woman's duty as "to diligently and thriftily build the nation."[74]

In agriculture among the mutual aid teams and cooperatives, there was a universal practice of giving women unequal pay for equal work with men. In a few mutual aid organizations, women were given no work points at all, while in a large number of organizations the remuneration of women's labor was arbitrarily fixed at half that of the men's.[75]

The acute need for labor precipitated by the Great Leap Forward policies at the end of 1958 forced the Communist Party to come to grips with the problem of women's domestic labor and the shortage of daycare facilities. The literature of this period once again emphasized the necessity for women to get into production. A radical attempt was made to communalize living, through mess halls, nurseries, and kindergartens.

"On International Women's Day, March 8, 1959, the *Jen-min jih-pao* (People's Daily) claimed that the drive of 'socializing household work' has set up in China 3,600,000 public mess halls and 4,980,000 nurseries and kindergartens staffed by some 7,000,000 women child-care workers. Thus freed from cooking, child care, and many other domestic chores now collectively performed, nearly '100 per cent' of all rural women have joined productive labor in the communes."[76]

By 1960, it was claimed that in the rural communes 80 percent of all preschool children were being taken care of. In the cities it was reported that there was a fiftyfold increase between 1957 and 1958 in kindergartens, taking care of 25.5 million children. Forty-seven million children were supposed to be under care of permanent child-care organizations. [77]

Since then the situation in childcare facilities has continued to improve, although the director of the Department of Women stated in 1965 that nurseries and schools for all, even for a few hours a day, would not be achieved for twenty years. [78]

There are currently three types of child care facilities: feeding stations for infants up to the age of one; nurseries for children between the ages of one and three; and kindergartens for those aged three to seven. The feeding stations are connected with work sites, and mothers are given time off work twice a day to feed their infants.

In 1971, 50 percent of all city children between the ages of one and three attended nurseries, while 10 percent were cared for by nonworking mothers, and the remaining 40 percent were looked after by grandparents, neighbors, or family friends. In that same year, over 80 percent of the children between the ages of three and seven in urban areas were attending kindergartens. [79]

The majority of childcare facilities are only open during the day, although there are a small number of twenty-four hour facilities, and some of the daycare centers take children for the evening hours if the parents have to attend meetings.

Twenty-four hour childcare can be costly in relative terms. The Pai Hai kindergarten in Peking, for example, costs 20.20 yuan per child per month, a significant portion of the average factory worker's 60 yuan per month salary. However, those unable to afford such childcare may be assisted financially by the factories where they work. In Canton, the twenty-four hour childcare centers are substantially cheaper, twelve yuan per child per month. [80]

Nurseries and kindergartens are generally quite simple, with few toys and rudimentary facilities. At some of the kindergartens, the children do small amounts of productive labor,[81] which obviously has a far greater symbolic than economic significance. Drama is an important part of the young people's day in kindergarten. Ruth Sidel offers some interesting comments on how the role of women is reflected in the skits the children act out. Describing her visit to a Shanghai kindergarten, she said:

"Two of the songs we heard at the Workers' Village Kindergarten, which are often sung during performances, can help clarify the current role of women as acted out by the children. In the first song, eight girls in blue shorts and white blouses danced into the room waving red flags and cardboard sabers and acted out a scene from the revolutionary ballet *The Red Detachment of Women* in which women are portrayed as fine soldiers committed to the revolutionary cause. The plot concerns a peasant girl from the island of Hainan who is beaten by the landlord's henchmen and left, hurt, in the forest. She is found by a detachment of revolutionaries, mainly women, and the remainder of the story tells of her maturing as a member of the detachment and their revenge on the landlord. The other song sung by the children and frequently heard is from *The White-haired Girl*— the scene in which male soldiers from the People's Liberation Army free a village and girls from the village offer the soldiers food and presents, indicating, as the interpreter told us, 'the close relationship between the people and the army.' These two views of women— fierce, militant, equal to men on the one hand, and traditional, food preparing, morale-giving supporter at home, on the other— are reflective of the society's larger view. And it is quite appropriate that children act out the larger society's views of the role of women, as they do in other areas."[82]

In the countryside there are fewer childcare facilities and they are organized more casually. The nurseries and kindergartens are often seasonal, operating during the harvest period or in other busy seasons. The facilities are more rudimentary than in the cities, often being a single room with less equipment than the city center has. These rural facilities are generally organized on the production team and production brigade levels rather than at the commune level. [83]

Communal mess halls, nurseries, and household services were also instituted in the cities along with city communes, but the hostility of the urban population to the drastic regimentation of their lives offset completely the progressive features of these institutions and they were soon abandoned. While they lasted, there was a big increase in female employment in the cities. Women industrial and office workers soared from 3 million in 1957 to 7.5 million in 1958. [84] One-and-a-half million housewives who did not hold regular jobs were reported to have set up small workshops, knitting mills, and foundries. [85] In some fields there were permanent gains. From 1957 to 1961, the number of women research technicians increased sixfold in Shanghai.

The failure of the communes flowed from the tasks they were designed to accomplish. The emancipation of female labor was not a central one. The Stalinist regime faced the problem of extending effective control down to the village level, something no previous government had ever succeeded in doing apart from tax collections and military repression. This became urgent as the cohesive peasant villages resisted state grain collections even after they had been "collectivized" in the 1955-57 period. As George Moseley reports, "Whereas per capita food consumption in urban areas declined slightly between 1953 and 1957, the rural population increased its per capita grain consumption by more than 10 per cent." [86]

It was the failure of the family-oriented, material-incentive program inherited from Soviet Stalinism that prompted Mao to seek more direct methods to assert party control at the village level. Thus the Maoist high tides, in the Great Leap Forward and again in the Cultural Revolution, combined a progressive attempt to free women to participate in productive labor by providing a dramatic extension of social services, with the attempt at the same time to curtail the peasant standard of living, and to impose a ruthless regimentation on the peasant population as a whole. This included a drastic lengthening of the work day and compulsory attendance at frequent and prolonged indoctrination and "self-criticism" sessions where dissent was located, isolated, and suppressed.

One measure of the increased labor was in the number of days worked per year. Peasant farm activity under the old regime had been brutally controlled by the landlords and rich peasants, but without state intervention to organize the construction of water conservancy projects the actual number of days worked per year was, as in any peasant economy, rather low compared to an industrial worker. Moseley gives the figures of 172 days per year for the average peasant in the 1920s, compared with 250 days per year in 1956. [87] Schran, using only Maoist statistical source material, reports that the number of work days jumped from 204 for men and 105 for women in 1957 in the advanced cooperatives (this leaves out time spent on private plots, which were initially abolished by the communes) to 336 days for men and 300 for women in the communes in 1958-59.[88]

In addition, many communes abolished money wages and substituted payment in kind. Socialism, of course, aspires to eliminate money and replace it with the free distribution of goods; but in the dire poverty of the Chinese countryside of 1958 or of today, eliminating cash only reduces the number of choices for peasants and workers who cannot then save up to buy consumer goods. This also had to be abandoned because of peasant opposition.

The militarization of the peasants' daily life is vividly depicted in the following account of life on a commune that appeared in a party magazine of the time.

"At daybreak, bells ring and whistles blow to assemble
. . . In about a quarter of an hour the peasants line
up. At the command of company and squad commanders,
the teams march to the fields, holding flags. Here one
no longer sees peasants in groups of two or three, smok-
ing and going leisurely to the fields. What one hears
are the sounds of measured steps and marching songs.
The desultory living habits which have been with the
peasants for thousands of years are gone forever . . .
Individualism has absolutely no market here."[89]

The militarization of life in the countryside led to the
de facto sit-down strikes discussed earlier that paralyzed
the economy and led to three years of terrible harvests.
The Stalinists were forced to retreat. While the communes
were not abandoned, their size, range of social services,
and range of social control over their members were
greatly reduced by 1959-60. Women were particularly
hard hit by the resulting economic dislocation and decrease of production, being the first to be released from
work. Communal eating facilities and day-care centers
were disbanded.[90] The burden of domestic work was
once again left up to the individual woman. The percentage of women in industry declined from 17 percent
in 1959 to 15 percent in 1966.[91]

To justify the firing of women and the turning back
of women's integration into production, all the reactionary ideology that had been traditionally used against
women surfaced in the party press. This was the Liu
Shao-ch'i period (1959-66), when the standards were
taken from the maudlin evocations of motherhood of
Stalinist Russia rather than from the school of spartan
subordination of self to party command more common
to Maoism.

The journal of the Women's Association, *Chung-kuo
fu-nü* (China's Women) in its last issue before ceasing
publication in 1966, when it had come back under Maoist
control, made a "self-criticism" of the editorial policy of

the previous six years. It quoted earlier articles that had "intoxicated women with the small heaven of motherhood, bearing children and managing family affairs." Women had been told that "to have a warm small family is happiness itself," and that to bear and nurture children is "women's natural duty." Articles had been published without criticism that bore titles like "Women Live for the Purpose of Raising Children" and "For Women to Engage in Enterprises is like Flying Kites Under the Bed." At the same time, the new line was suggested by the editorial's attack on the "bourgeois and revisionist fallacy" that "there must be 'common feelings and interests' in selecting lovers [spouses]." [92]

A widely studied handbook, *Love, Marriage, and the Family*, published by the Maoist faction on the eve of the Cultural Revolution in 1964, stressed a "real-life episode" as a model for young people in which a young educated woman from the city proves her devotion to the party by cementing her decision to spend her whole life working as a peasant by marrying a near-illiterate peasant youth. This was later made into a film and given wide circulation. [93]

The Cultural Revolution reemphasized the need for women to work outside the home, and recent reports from visitors to China indicate that the vast majority of women now are working. On the rural communes visited in the summer of 1971 by the Committee of Concerned Asian Scholars, all the women were working with the exception of old women with bound feet. [94] Ruth Sidel was told in the fall of 1971 that 90 percent of all Chinese women worked outside the home, including those in the countryside. [95] How many of them work full time and year round is, however, hard to determine. In some areas of China many women are still used as a reserve labor force to work during busy seasons such as harvest time and then return to the home. In other cases women are involved only in sideline production done in their spare time. [96] In addition, the proportion of women to men employed in industry remains low. Janet Salaff, a University of Toronto professor, estimates that by 1972 the proportion of women workers in industry had only reached the 1957 level of 17 percent. [97]

Clearly defined sexual roles, which are accepted rather than fought, still exist in the Chinese economy. The care of children, for example, is still seen as women's work, and all nursery and kindergarten teachers are women. Ruth Sidel comments that "there seems to be no effort to recruit men into fields in which they would be dealing with small children. And there seems to be no concern for breaking down the traditional sex roles in professions such as teaching and nursing, both of which are virtually all female." She went on to state that "our interpreter and . . . the secretary general of the Chinese Medical Association, with whom we discussed this point, both felt that sex-determined job preferences were natural; after all the sexes are different and might well wish to enter different fields." [98]

Members of the Committee of Concerned Asian Scholars also noticed this perpetuation of sexual roles in employment. They wrote that while women predominate in the teaching of the lower grades, the higher up one goes on the educational ladder, the smaller the percentage of women gets. By the time you get to the university faculties, men form a solid majority. At Peking University, for example, there are 1,487 men and 646 women on the faculty. This means that "the most prestigious and highly paid jobs" in the educational system "are still heavily male." [99]

In the textile industry, the work force is no longer virtually totally female, as it was before the revolution. The men who now work in the industry, however, are concentrated in certain jobs. The CCAS described the situation in two textile mills they visited. At one the work force is 20 percent male, and at the other it is 40 percent male. As they walked around the factories, the Western visitors noticed "that in all highly mechanized tasks the men and women work together side by side doing the same thing. But wherever a job has not been mechanized, the task is done by women. At the textile mill the only tedious task still done by hand is the final inspection of every foot of cloth produced and the hand repairs of all flaws in the cloth, and the workers who do this are all women. At the embroidery factory, some pictures are still totally hand-sewn, with each picture requiring nearly two months of careful work. Only women do this work." [100]

At the heavy industrial installations they visited, they noticed that the vast majority of employees were men. At a factory manufacturing railroad rolling stock, for example, only 1,700 of the 9,000 workers were women. This included women employed to care for the children in the nurseries, kindergartens, and primary schools attached to the plant. [101]

One of China's most important institutions is the People's Liberation Army, which plays a very major role in the economic and political life of the country. PLA members hold high administrative positions in virtually every area of Chinese life. For that reason, the fact that women play no significant role in the army bars them from equality in leadership roles in Chinese society as a whole. Women in the PLA are mostly involved in logistics, medical, and office work.

In general there appears to be little consciousness regarding the sexual determination of employment roles. When the Concerned Asian Scholars "asked why these differences between male and female employment continue," they "were usually told that women are by nature better suited to some tasks, such as gentle care of the sick, patient rearing of children, and meticulous sewing or inspection tasks where perfection is required." "Neither the men nor the women," according to the Asian scholars, "seemed to question the assumption that there are these sorts of inherent differences between men and women." [102]

The sexual determination of roles is most pronounced in the unpaid household labor. There the patriarchal division of labor inherited from the old system has been most resistant to change. The Committee of Concerned Asian Scholars report that everywhere in China they asked questions about who cleaned house, washed clothes, took care of children, did the shopping, cooked the meals, did the sewing. The answer was almost invariably "The wife, of course."[103]

Wages in industry, which affects only a small majority of Chinese women, are relatively equal between the sexes. On the communes, however, women receive fewer work points than men because they are judged to be weaker and have to do housework, which is unpaid. And unlike their urban counterparts, commune women do not receive any pay when on maternity leaves. [104]

In the spring of 1971 the West German scholar Klaus Mehnert visited China as a personal friend of Prince Sihanouk of Cambodia. He spent some time at Tachai, the model production brigade visited each year by millions of Chinese peasants as the example to strive after in their own localities. He noted that there were ten pay categories at Tachai, ranging from ten work points a day for a strong man to seven for the most productive single woman, to six-and-a-half for a married woman. The weak or unproductive are paid less. The differences are quite substantial. A man in the top category received 450 yuan per year (U.S. $180) compared to 300 yuan (U.S. $120) for the top female wage earners. He questioned two of the women leaders at Tachai on this discrepancy.

"'In my country,' I said, 'we battled a hundred years for women to have equal pay for equal work. Don't you find it an injustice to be paid so much less?'

"'But a married woman devotes much of her working energy to her family,' they answered. 'Those are individual chores. Should the collective have to pay for work not done in the service of the collective?'"[105]

Mehnert writes that he saw unmarried women doing all kinds of the heaviest work. And yet, since women are not supposed to be as strong as men, they were paid less. Ken Dawson, a New Zealand engineer and a member of the Socialist Action League in that country, visited China in April 1973 and reported that "women are given on the average two-thirds of the work points of men. The work points are not just related to the work performed, but also to sex. Regardless of how good a worker you were, if you were a female, you just didn't get into a certain work-point bracket."[106]

WOMEN IN MANAGEMENT

After the revolution, women for the first time began to take administrative positions in the factories. This radically conflicted with the old Confucian traditions of women's submission to men. Hugo Portisch describes in his *Red China Today* a textile factory he visited in Peking in 1965, where the majority of workers were female and every member of the management, including the factory director, was a woman.[107]

The most extensive report on the administrative structure of Chinese industry is the work done by Canadian management consultant Barry M. Richman after a two-month investigation at thirty-five major Chinese factories in May and June of 1966. He had previously conducted a similar survey of sixteen factories in the Soviet Union and his direct comparisons add interest to his Chinese observations. It is true that this was before the Cultural Revolution, but it was almost twenty years after the CCP came to power so that certain trends are clearly evident and there are no indications that the position of women has qualitatively changed in the intervening years.

First, Richman raises the problem of educational qualification for management positions. He writes:

"In 1960 in the Soviet Union there were over 129,000

women engaged in scientific research, 30,000 of them having the equivalent of doctoral or master's degrees, and 700 the title of professor. In Communist China in 1963 there were fewer than 200 females having the equivalent of a Ph.D. and not many more having the equivalent of a master's degree."[108]

Granted that the Soviet Union is far more economically advanced than China. But even though the USSR is also a Stalinist regime that glorifies the family the opportunities for women's economic advancement are greatly disproportionate to those in China. In 1965, for example, the Soviet Union produced three times as much pig iron as China, seven times as much cement, ten times as much electric power, but 150 times as many highly educated women.[109]

Richman, while in the Soviet Union, observed that "women constituted 45 percent of all managers and staff specialists at Soviet industrial enterprises in the late 1950's, but only 12 percent of the top management positions at Soviet enterprises of all types were held by women." At the sixteen Soviet enterprises he visited, he counted two female directors and two women chief engineers. He adds, "I did not come across any in Chinese industry. . . . I was introduced to six or seven female vice directors — out of a total of about eighty or ninety — in Chinese industry, and only one of them was employed by a heavy-industry plant."[110]

He summed up his observations:

"Roughly 15 percent of the department heads and 10 percent of the workshop directors whom I encountered in Chinese industry were female. And again most of these women managers were employed by consumer-goods producers. In general, the proportion of female lower-level managers, particularly floor foremen or group leaders, was substantially higher than higher-level female managers. In some light-industry firms 50 percent or more of the lower-level managers were female, and in a few cases the vast majority of the group leaders were women.

"In general, there seem to be ample opportunities for female employees to become lower-level managers in Chinese industry, and fairly numerous opportunities to make it to the middle-management level. As a female approaches the top ranges of the executive hierarchy, however, there seem to be substantially fewer opportunities for promotion."[111]

We must remember that this is an extremely centralized society, where appointments to directorships are made as much on the basis of party-administrative experience as on the basis of particular knowledge of the industrial process. The CCP hierarchy has jealously guarded its control of state government and economic enterprises. If there are few or almost no women in administrative positions this reflects conscious leadership decisions in cadre selection in the CCP going back forty years and more, rather than only economic backwardness or prejudices of the male masses.

WOMEN IN POLITICS

In the first years of the Maoist regime, a big drive was launched to involve women in the political life of China. This was no simple process. *Hsin Chung-kuo fu-nu* in in December 1951 published an article entitled "Beating, Scolding and Mistreatment of Women Should Not be Allowed to Continue," which recounted the conditions women activists faced:

"Some women who participated in the women's association, in literacy classes, or in newspaper-reading groups, have come home to confront the long faces of a husband and mother-in-law. Some women have returned from a meeting and the family would not give them food to eat, and some have even been locked out of the house. Some husbands and mothers-in-law summarily forbid women from participating in any social activity. Still other women are beaten up or even tortured to death by their husbands and mothers-in-law because of participation in social activities."[112]

Women used some unique ways to counter the resistance. Belden cites a case in the village of Tinghu where in the first election the chief was chosen without any of the women having voted. Many women said they would not recognize him as the chief—but the men just laughed. The women then refused to sleep with their husbands — and finally the men surrendered and called a new election. A woman was elected as vice-chief of the village and another became head of the Education Bureau.113

At the lower levels, women's involvement in the political life of the country dramatically increased. Of the local deputies of the People's Congress, women composed 10 percent in 1951, increasing to 20 percent by 1956.114 Women occupied from 10 to 15 percent of the posts of committee member, chairman, or vice-chairman of the peasant associations.115 There were some women deputy directors or even full directors, in two-thirds of the Agricultural Producers' Cooperatives throughout the country in 1957.[116] In 1951, women comprised 8 percent of the lower level functionaries; by 1955 this had risen to 14.5 percent.[117] They played a decisive role in the residents committees in urban centers, although these had rather limited responsibilities, looking after sanitation, welfare work, culture, and recreation.118 As C.K. Yang put it:

"That common women such as laborers and peasants now hold responsible positions as a regular part of the political system is striking evidence of the new situation brought about by the changed social status of women under Communist rule."119

* The changes have been dramatic, although we should not lose sight of the fact that the Stalinist CCP invites participation in politics only on the condition that there is unquestioning agreement with its policies. Undoubtedly this is a great step forward from complete exclusion from public life. But dissent of any kind, by men or women, is met by social ostracism, loss of jobs, or deportation to labor reform farms in the rural areas for indefinite sentences.

Even within the framework of the politics of the ruling privileged bureaucratic caste, the position of politically conformist women has not been a steady upward advance. In the early part of 1958 there was retrenchment in the ranks of urban cadres (this was repeated in the second Maoist high tide in the Cultural Revolution). Many were dismissed and it was the women who were most likely to be let go. The Communist Party sought to mobilize women into the labor force during the Great Leap Forward, but it did not encourage women to take on political responsibilities. This failure of the CCP to carry a sustained campaign against the traditional barriers to women's involvement in political administration resulted in only a small proportion of women assuming leadership positions. In 1960, women were only around 10 percent of the brigade leaders and 5 percent of the commune leaders. A woman interviewed by Janet Salaff a number of years later told her:

"Before the Cultural Revolution women seldom went out to work as cadres. They dared not do so, for their parents preferred them to stay at home to do the housework or work in the fields. The elders did not understand that any work for the brigades would be remunerated in work points."[120]

With the shakeup of the bureaucracy during the Cultural Revolution and Mao's use of mass forces to destroy opposition within the party, a new drive was opened to bring women under the CCP's political influence and to push back the contrary pressures of the family that had been encouraged by Liu Shao-ch'i. Women were urged to use Mao's works to criticize domineering family members such as parents-in-law or husbands. More women assumed rural leadership positions. Jan Myrdal reported that in the village of Liu Ling women during the Cultural Revolution forced the adoption of a rule that women should have the same rights as men to go to a meeting — not just formally but in practice. On evenings when women went to meetings, men were obliged to look after the children.[121]

But women still remained very much in the minority in political organizations. In one district of Anhwei province, which was singled out for public praise for the number of women appointed to political positions, only 10 percent of the membership of the Revolutionary Committees were women. [122] The only area where women play a dominant political role is at the local level — in the lane committees of the cities. These committees provide health and social services and organize the block, but they make no significant political decisions. [123]

Recent reports indicate that at all other levels women are still greatly underrepresented. For example, while women comprised 40 percent of the enrollment at the Peking Cadre School in 1971, only five of the twenty-three members of the school's Revolutionary Committee were women, and only one of the nine members of the school's Communist Party committee was a woman.

In the more advanced rural communes, women may make up as much as one-third of the leadership groups. But even those women who are leaders find their roles confined. Their jobs are mainly to organize other women and carry out the decisions of higher bodies made up predominantly of men. [124]

One major problem in the participation of women in political activity is that the percentage of women in the Communist Party and the PLA, the two major sources from which the leadership of local bodies is chosen, is extremely low. As of 1961, the last year for which information on the CCP's social composition is available, women constituted only about 10 percent of the total party membership. [125] And the proportion of women in the PLA is even lower.

As a result, although the elected members of a factory or city Revolutionary Committee might include women, these committees also include members of the PLA and Communist Party assigned to lead the committee, and these members are usually all men. This means that the inbalance between men and women is further exacerbated by the inbalance in the PLA and CCP.

The low proportion of women in the CCP extends vertically throughout the organization. In the higher echelons the position of women has scarcely changed from the 1950s, and the proportion of women remains extremely low. The Central Committee elected by the Eighth Congress of the CCP in 1956 included 70 males and 4 females, meaning that women comprised 5.4 percent of that body's membership. The Ninth Central Committee, elected in 1969, was made up of 134 males and 11 females, meaning that women were slightly less than 8 percent of the membership. This relative exclusion from "the seat of ideological and political control" as Ai-li S. Chin put it, suggests that "equality of sex does not really extend to matters of central importance."[126]

There is a disturbing trend even among those few women who do get to the top in the CCP. The two women on the Political Bureau after 1969, Yeh Chun and Chiang Ching, were never independent political figures but rather rose to power through their marriages with Mao Tse-tung and Lin Piao. Wang Kuang-mei, another important political figure, saw her career rise and fall with that of her husband, Liu Shao-ch'i. The purge of Lin Piao in September 1971 led to the downfall of Yeh Chun as well, leaving only Chiang Ching near the top. At the Tenth Party Congress in August 1973 there were still no women elected to the Political Bureau Standing Committee.

ABORTION, BIRTH CONTROL, AND SEXUALITY

The Chinese woman's traditional role was confined to that of breeder, her status being defined by that alone. Now with the breakdown of the precapitalist family and kinship system and woman's integration into productive life she has begun to transcend that role. But essential to woman's equal participation in the overall life of the nation is her control over her biology. Thus of utmost importance to the Chinese woman is the question of distribution and knowledge of birth control. What has been the Communist Party's policy in this sphere?

The official thinking on birth control has almost never been expressed in direct statements and proclamations. Nevertheless, some very definite trends can be noted. In determining its policy on this question, the Communist Party hierarchy seems to have completely disregarded as a consideration the right of women to control their own bodies. Administrative prescriptions for population needs are the sole criteria used.

Birth control was ignored in the first few years of CCP power. Population growth, it was said, was not a problem. It seems that the situation even deteriorated in these years. An editorial in the Peking *Kuang jih pao* in August 1956 reported that in some pharmaceutical plants the production of contraceptives had been stopped. It also noted that drug stores would neither sell nor show contraceptives to women. [127]

The spiraling population growth prompted a change in policy in 1956 and a mass birth-control campaign was launched. The Ministry of Health demanded that medical and public health organizations at various levels assume the burden of informing people about contraceptives, and that provincial and municipal departments train groups to give such guidance. Abortion was also favored as a technique of birth control. Abortion and sterilization both became easily available in the years 1956-57. [128]

There was some resistance from peasants who associated offspring with security for their old age. But there seems also to have been a definite demand from women for the devices. A member of the Women's Federation reported that they had to initiate the campaign cautiously or there might have been a flood of requests that they could not have met. [129]

In May 1958, the birth-control campaign was abruptly called off. The CCP in its Great Leap Forward policy contradictorily called on women both to participate fully in the labor force and at the same time to reproduce at a heightened rate. It was argued that the strength and wealth of China lay in its population. [130] Abortion and sterilization were discouraged, although still permitted on the advice of a doctor. [131]

With the failure of the Great Leap Forward and the sharp decline in Mao's authority in the central leadership, a renewed effort began to disseminate birth-control information and devices. In 1965, 1,000 mobile medical teams were sent out across the country, one of their main tasks being the promotion of birth control. The results of one team that visited Jen-ho, a commune near Canton, give an indication of the scope of the campaign.

Jen-ho had a population of 53,000 people. The team spent four months there, training 450 people who would be able to continue the work after the team left. Some 8,800 people participated in their propaganda meetings, which made use of plays and skits as well as speeches. More than 10,000 people saw films on birth control and 8,000 pamphlets and books were distributed. The team performed 48 abortions, 547 IUD insertions, and 18 sterilizations in its short stay. In addition, 3,475 birth-control kits were given out to the commune members.[132]

Except for a brief period during the Cultural Revolution, the Chinese government's policy toward birth control has remained favorable. To get birth control now, a woman has only to call at the village clinic and she is given a free supply of pills or other devices. A great deal of research has gone into finding safe, simple methods of contraception that can be dispensed by lower-level health personnel. One method for abortions is the fire-suction bottle, which works on the principle of the vacuum aspirator, and which can be used in rural areas without electricity.[133] Abortions throughout the country are free, available on request of the woman alone, and are usually performed within fifty days of conception. If a woman has an early abortion, she is allowed ten days off work. If for some reason the abortion is not performed until after fifty days of pregnancy, and this is not usual, she is given one month off.

The effectiveness of the birth-control campaigns can be seen in the low birthrates in Chinese cities. Shanghai, for example, has a birthrate of 6-7 per thousand per year, much lower than the U.S. birthrate of 17 per thousand per year. In rural areas where old attitudes are more deeply entrenched, however, the birthrate is much higher. Nonetheless, there is no question but that the government birth-control campaigns have made a significant impact.[134]

But birth control and abortion are not seen as a means of freeing women's sexuality. They are strictly used in the context of population planning. In contrast to the early stages of the Russian Revolution, the advances women made in marriage and property rights were not accompanied by a liberation of female sexuality.

An extreme puritanism characterizes the CCP's "line" on sexuality. K.S. Karol, who lived in the Soviet Union from 1939 to the end of World War II and visited China on the eve of the Cultural Revolution, found China more sexually repressive than Stalinist Russia. He noted that kissing wasn't allowed on the screen in Chinese films and that literature on love relationships skirted the whole problem of sexuality. Karol had some interesting comments on the CCP's sexual code after an interview with a particularly officious film maker in Shanghai:

"Our film-makers' arguments in favor of the Maoist mora code would . . . be difficult to refute if the choice in this sphere was only between this and the previous [Confucian] code. But the neo-puritan side of Maoism is self-evident and offends so much more because it is taught not only in the countryside but also in the towns, where the traditions to be countered are not at all the same. Since before the war, millions of urban Chinese have broken with the partiarchal family concept. [The film Karol had been shown limited its advice on sex to opposing arranged marriages.] . . .

"Admittedly, we can't know how the regime's moralistic regulations are applied in Shanghai. . . . Behind the rigid facade of official puritanism there exists, perhaps, a certain semiclandestine freedom of morals comparable to that which I knew in Stalin's Russia. This idea often struck me because the Maoist family directives are very much like those the Soviet regime lavished on us and which we applied, it must be admitted, with a minimum of discipline. But China is no doubt better organized and even more rigid than the U.S.S.R. was. 'Dissolute morals' are condemned here without appeal, and adultery is punished by law, which was never the case in Russia."135

Elsewhere, Karol describes the sexual regime in the universities he visited:

"Boys and girls often live on different floors of the same building, but flirtations and affairs are so severely frowned on by the authorities that infringements of this rule can lead to expulsion."[136]

Karol, it must be noted, frames his criticisms in a context of the highest praise for the Maoist regime.

Helen Snow, in her *Women in Modern China,* admits the puritanism but claims that it is part of an attempt by women to demand respect for themselves. It is true that many of the measures taken against exploitative relationships such as concubinage, prostitution, and rape are highly progressive. But there is another side to this problem. Puritanism historically has been used as a tool against women; their sexuality has been repressed, while men have had various socially sanctioned outlets for their sexual expression. There is evidence that a double standard remains in China, and, because it is a male-dominated society, it is likely to persist. One man in an interview with Janet Salaff in 1969 made the following comments:

"Most of the men of the village play around with girls. They leave behind girls with whom they have sexual relations and change to others. Thus no matter how high a position a daughter holds, others will say 'what's so good about that, she also plays around with boys.' This affects the parents' reputation, and they may not be able to marry out their daughters so they prevent their daughters from working in the commune or the brigade."[137]

What kind of caricature of socialism is it where who one sleeps with is the business of the ruling party and the police? What kind of respect for women is it when denunciations by an informer can lose her a job, deny her an education, or send her to a labor camp? It would be a small comfort to think that such laws were equally enforced to stifle the private lives of both men and women. But is even that likely to be true? In a society where a privileged bureaucratic caste is in power, where the officialdom at every level is dominated by males, where women by virtue of their liability to pregnancy are more likely to reveal their transgression than men, isn't it going to be women, and the least educated and least powerful at that, who are going to have to face the repressive arm of the state in the enforcement of these antisexual laws? Trotsky described the introduction of similar reactionary laws in the Soviet Union by Stalin as "the philosophy of a priest endowed also with the powers of a gendarme."

SOME CONCLUSIONS

The Chinese revolution that shattered the military power of capitalism in 1949 and destroyed the capitalist economy in 1953 dealt a powerful blow to the age-old forces that held Chinese women in subjugation. The traditional patriarchal clan system in the villages stood as an insurmountable barrier to female emancipation, condemning women to a lifetime of household slavery. That system was swept away.

The emergence of women into productive and political life was an absolutely essential precondition for genuine sexual equality and the advance toward a truly human society of abundance and freedom under socialism. These are accomplishments that must be recognized in the Chinese revolution and defended against external attacks by imperialism that could only end in a restoration of the system of female slavery that prevails in every one of the underdeveloped capitalist countries in the world.

We must also recognize that even with the best intentions and the greatest encouragement to female political leadership there are grave limitations placed on the potential accomplishments of a socialist revolution in a backward country. The family cannot be abolished. As

82

long as a society is too poor to provide adequate child care, communal laundries, and good quality communal food services, the burdens of raising children will fall on the individual family, and hence, largely on women.

Given these limitations, however, we must ask whether the policies of the party in power promote the emancipation of women or act to prevent it. It is clear that a deeply rooted sexual inequality remains in China today. Women are subject to both job discrimination and, in their majority — peasant women — to unequal wages. Their involvement in production has by no means been a steady uphill climb; they are the first to be sent back to the home in a period of economic slump. The regime has not consistently placed a high priority or sometimes any priority on the creation of child-care centers, with the result that women continue to bear a double burden even when they do hold jobs outside the home. Women continue to face the conflict between domestic labor and child rearing on one side and opportunities to participate equally with men in the productive and political sphere.

While there was a considerable increase in women's political participation in the first few years of the revolution, the pace was not continued. At the lower levels, fewer than 20 percent of the administrative positions are filled by women. In the top levels of the hierarchy, the proportion is much lower and, in essence, women have no real power at the top except through their husbands.

A double standard still exists and women suffer most from the repressive sexual mores. The price women must pay for the right to have sex is marriage and acceptance of the role of domestic laborer. Organized social pressure against divorce and legal sanctions against sex outside of marriage act to keep women in many marriages that in a less restrictive society would be rejected as oppressive.

Birth control and abortion are freely available, and of great benefit for women. But inasmuch as the Communist Party does not recognize the democratic right of women to have control over their bodies, these benefits remain shaky.

Many rationalizations have been used to justify the continuing inequality of women and the subordination of women's rights to the needs of the regime. Most of these center on the claim that individual freedom must be sacrificed to increase industrial production so that a future generation can enjoy the benefits that abundance will make possible. Dubious as this argument is in the sphere of consumption, it has no bearing at all on the prohibition of nonmarital sex and the severe restrictions on divorce, which aim at *bolstering the nuclear family*, not at increasing social productivity. On the contrary this reactionary policy reduces the political and productive potential of women, who make up 48 percent of the members of Chinese society.

These contradictions cannot be explained by simply referring to the economic backwardness of China, or even to the survival of male chauvinist prejudices among CCP leaders. Such explanations assume that time by itself will overcome these obstacles and that the present regime, whatever its weaknesses, is moving forward toward a society of socialist freedom. On the contrary, Stalinism is a thoroughly retrograde phenomenon in the workers' movement. In the Soviet Union the rise of Stalin marked the consolidation of a conservative, antidemocratic privileged bureaucratic caste. This caste was duplicated in China by the CCP. The Cultural Revolution, while exposing some of the privileges of the bureaucracy, led to no fundamental changes in the regime. During that period Mao demagogically denounced the bureaucracy, calling for the creation of democratic and egalitarian institutions modeled on the Paris Commune.

But Mao had no intention of leading a struggle for

socialist democracy. Quite the contrary! His appeals to the masses were designed solely to destroy the political dominance of a rival sector of the bureaucratic caste, led by the Liu Shao-ch'i faction in the CCP. Once he had toppled his rivals, and threatened by the dynamic of the mass mobilizations he had encouraged, Mao called on the PLA to maintain control. Hundreds of Red Guard units were demobilized and their radicalized members were sent into the countryside to be "reeducated" by the peasantry. The bureaucrats continued to control the lives and destiny of the Chinese people.

The scope of the privileges of this bureaucratic caste is hinted at in a letter published on the front page of the *People's Daily* in Peking in January 1974. This letter is a self-criticism by the son of a leading cadre of the Political Department of the Foochow units of the PLA. He confesses that his father had used his influence to get him into college while the rest of his generation was being sent off to the countryside. He further stated:

"I did not mind a bit when I lost a watch worth more than 400 yuan. My father later bought me another watch worth more than 180 yuan. I live a lavish life and do not aim high politically. If I do not mend my ways, I shall become a renegade to our revolutionary forefathers." [138]

Since a skilled worker is paid 400 yuan for six months work and a peasant must work nearly an entire year to earn that much, it is a telling indication of the privileges the bureaucracy receives that it can afford such watches for its children. What a far cry this is from the goals of the Paris Commune, where state officials were to be paid no more than workers' wages.

The Chinese bureaucracy seeks to defend its powers and privileges against the working class and other oppressed sectors of society by accomodations with world capitalism in its foreign policy and by strengthening reactionary social institutions at home.

This pattern is not new for the CCP. It goes back to

the period of its Stalinization in the late 1920s. The embryo of the authoritarian social relations it fostered after it took power was evident in the period before the revolution as well. The experiences of women CP intellectuals such as Ting Ling throw some interesting light on the CCP's long-standing attitude toward women.

Ting Ling was a leader of the women's rights movement, a member of the CCP, and one of its most prominent writers. In the early 1950s she received the Stalin prize for her novel *The Sun Shines on San Kan River*. In 1942 in an article entitled "Thoughts on March 8th," she raised some sharp criticisms of the official CCP leadership, revealing the difficulties and disillusionment of women living at the Maoist capital of Yenan. Women, she wrote, were supposedly emancipated but remained subject to inequality and contempt. If women did not marry, they were ridiculed; if they did, they were chastized for holding political posts rather than being home with their families; if they remained in the house for a number of years, they were slandered as being backward. Whereas in the old society they were pitied by the CCP leadership, in the new they were condemned for a predicament not of their own making.

She described Yenan as a place where certain groups had privileges over others. She admitted that the position of women in Yenan was better than elsewhere. But it did not measure up to the theories the CCP proclaimed about equal rights. She blamed particularly the top party leaders for empty promises and lack of action. Men in important positions, she declared, "should talk less of meaningless theories and talk more of actual problems." For this she was forced to undergo "thought reform."[139] Her "reformed" attitudes afterwards, indicating the CCP's official attitude toward feminism, were reported by a journalist who interviewed her:

"She admitted to him that her problem and that of some women was that they still had the same attitudes they had formed in the man-centered society of old China. In

Yenan there was equality of sexes; *she had now realized her narrow feminism was outdated. Instead of improving cooperation between men and women and all social groups she had caused disunity.*[140] (Emphasis added.)

Women could criticize the male authority structures as much as they liked as long as it applied to the old system. But a word against the authoritarian structures of the Maoist regime was met with reprisals. In 1957 Ting Ling was purged from the party for speaking out during the "Hundred Flowers Bloom" episode against the party's line on love and marriage.

The repressive defense by the Stalinists of the nuclear family, and with it of female oppression, flows not primarily from the lack of funds for social services to replace it. If that were the case, economic necessity alone would hold the family together until it could be replaced. The coercive attitudes of the CCP toward sexuality and divorce stem rather from the need to defend hierarchical privilege against democratic and egalitarian demands by the masses.

Wilhelm Reich, the well-known psychoanalyst who tried to develop a Marxian social psychology, discussed the implications of the profamily and antisexual policies of Soviet Stalinism:

"The repression of the sexual needs creates a general weakening of intellectual and emotional functioning; in particular, it makes people lack independence, will power and critical faculties. Authoritarian society is not concerned about morality per se. Rather, the anchoring of sexual morality and the changes it brings about in the organism create the specific psychic structure which forms the mass psychological basis of any authoritarian regime."[141] He added:

"The patriarchal family is the structural and ideological place of reproduction of every social order based on authoritarian principles."[142]

Leon Trotsky made a more concrete and scathing criticism of the antisocialist attitudes toward women and the family adopted by the Stalinist bureaucracy in the USSR. It could be applied just as well to Maoism today. He wrote:

"Instead of openly saying, 'We have proven still too poor and ignorant for the creation of socialist relations among men, our children and grandchildren will realize this aim', the leaders are forcing people to glue together again the shell of the broken family, and not only that, but to consider it, under threat of extreme penalties, the sacred nucleus of triumphant socialism. . . . A campaign is opened against too frequent and easy divorces. . . . The marriage and family laws established by the October revolution, once the object of its legitimate pride, are being made over and mutilated by vast borrowings from the law treasuries of the bourgeois countries. And as though on purpose to stamp treachery with ridicule, the same arguments which were earlier advanced in favor of unconditional freedom of divorce and abortion — 'the liberation of women,' 'defense of the rights of personality,' 'protection of motherhood' — are repeated now in favor of their limitation and complete prohibition. . . .

"The most compelling motive of the present cult of the family is undoubtedly the need of the bureaucracy for a stable hierarchy of relations, and for the disciplining of youth by means of 40,000,000 points of support for authority and power." [143]

The full emancipation of women in China will come only with the end of all authoritarian, hierarchal regimes that depend for their existence on relations of mastery and subordination. The achievements that have been made thus far must be defended and safeguarded, but the CCP will not and cannot carry them forward. That can be done only by the creation of institutions of mass socialist democracy that put an end to privilege. The CCP opposes by force the creation of such institutions.

The road to liberation lies in the independent mobilization of the Chinese masses, who through a political revolution will sweep away and destroy the ruling bureaucracy. This, combined with the extension of the world revolution, will usher in a period when society is cleansed of all sexism. It will herald the end of woman's age-old oppression, freeing her from the jail of the family institution, lifting the bars of archaic prejudices, and unleashing her full creative talents for the benefit of the entire society.

NOTES

1. William Goode, *World Revolution and Family Patterns* (Free Press of Glencoe, 1963), p. 281.
2. Francis Hsu, *Under the Ancestors' Shadow* (Columbia University Press, 1958), p. 123.
3. Francis Conway, "Women in the Chinese Revolution," *Fourth International,* July-August 1951, p. 110.
4. Jack Belden, *China Shakes the World* (Monthly Review Press, 1970), p. 155
5. Lin Yutang, *My Country and My People* (Halycon House, 1928), p. 154.
6. Laura Landy, *Women in the Chinese Revolution* (International Socialists, n.d.), p. 10.
7. Olga Lang, *Chinese Family and Society* (Yale University Press, 1946), p. 108.
8. Mary B. Rankin, *Early Chinese Revolutionaries* (Harvard University Press, 1971), pp. 40-44.
9. Mary C. Wright, ed., *China in Revolution: The First Phase* (Yale University Press, 1968), pp. 33-34.
10. Janet Weitzner Salaff and Judith Merkle, "Women and Revolution: The Lessons of the Soviet Union and China," *Socialist Revolution,* July-August 1970, p. 58.
11. Lang, pp. 109-110.
12. Chow Tse-tung, *The May Fourth Movement* (Harvard University Press, 1964), p. 258.
13. Helen Snow, *The Chinese Labor Movement* (John Day, 1964), p. 154.
14. Landy, p. 14.
15. Helen Snow, *The Chinese Communists* (Stanford University Press, 1952), pp. 235-6.
16. Quoted by Caroline Lund, "Women in the Chinese Revolution," *International Socialist Review,* June 1970, p. 13.
17. *Ibid.*
18. Snow, *The Chinese Communists,* p. 202.
19. Goode, pp. 275-276.
20. Harold R. Isaacs, *The Tragedy of the Chinese Revolution* (Stanford University Press, 1961), p. 31.
21. Helen Snow, *Inside Red China* (Doubleday, 1939).
22. Quoted in Allan S. Whiting, *Soviet Policies in China, 1917-1924* (Columbia University Press, 1954), p. 241.

23. Snow, *Inside Red China,* p. 170.
24. Helen Snow, *Women in Modern China* (Morton & Co., 1960), p. 242.
25. Snow, *The Chinese Communists,* p. 244.
26. William Hinton, *Fanshen* (Monthly Review Press, 1967), p. 457.
27. *Ibid.,* p. 397.
28. Salaff and Merkle, pp. 61-62.
29. Soon Ching Ling, *The Struggle for New China* (Foreign Languages Press, 1953), pp. 154-155.
30. Belden, p. 302.
31. Snow, *Women in Modern China,* p. 63.
32. Goode, p. 307.
33. *Ibid.,* p. 282.
34. The right of divorce was, however, restricted for wives of army personnel. They could only obtain a divorce with their husband's permission. (On this see M.J. Mejer, *Marriage Laws and Policy* (Hong Kong University Press, 1971), p. 82).
35. Conway, p. 112.
36. *The Marriage Law of the People's Republic of China* (Foreign Languages Press, 1950), p. 28.
37. Chang Chih-jang in *ibid.,* p. 18.
38. Teng Ying-chao in *ibid.,* p. 31.
39. C.K. Yang, *The Chinese Family in the Communist Revolution* (MIT Press, 1959), p. 201.
40. *The Marriage Law . . . ,* pp. 32-33.
41. Helen Snow, *Women in Modern China,* p. 13.
42. *Ibid.,* p. 23; and Ai-li S. Chin, "Mainland China," in *Women in the Modern World,* ed. by Raphael Patai (Free Press).
43. *The Marriage Law . . . ,* p. 38.
44. Yang, p. 36.
45. Goode, p. 277.
46. *Ibid.*
47. Cited by Yang, p. 136.
48. Hsia Kuang, "The Vicissitudes of the *Popular Pictorial Edition of the Marriage Law,*" *Hsin Chung-kuo fu-nu,* October 1955, cited by Yang, p. 210.
49. Yang, pp. 210-212.
50. Ai-li S. Chin, "Family Relations in Modern Chinese Fiction," in *Family and Kinship in Chinese Society* (Stanford University Press, 1970), p. 106.
51. George Moseley, *China Since 1911* (Harper & Row, 1968), p. 144.

92 *Women in China*

52. Chin, "Family Relations . . . ," p. 118.
53. Jan Myrdal, *Report From a Chinese Village* (Pantheon, 1965), pp. 26-27.
54. Chin, "Mainland China," p. 417.
55. Yang, p. 115.
56. Snow, *Women in Modern China,* p. 25.
57. Janet Salaff, *Tilling the Land for the Revolution: The Implications of the Ideology of Equality for Women's Fertility Goals in China,* unpublished draft of Ph. D. thesis.
58. Snow, *Women in Modern China,* p. 25.
59. Ross Terrill, *800,000,000: The Real China* (Little, Brown and Company, 1972), pp. 120-121.
60. Committee of Concerned Asian Scholars, *China! Inside the People's Republic* (Bantam, 1972), p. 273.
61. A. Linda Gordon, "The Fourth Mountain: Women in China," *Working Papers for a New Society,* Fall, 1973.
62. *Far Eastern Economic Review,* November 21, 1957.
63. Yang, p. 145.
64. *Far Eastern Economic Review.*
65. Snow, *Women in Modern China,* p. 177.
66. Goode, p. 304.
67. Cited by Peter Schran in *The Development of Chinese Agriculture, 1950-1959* (University of Illinois Press, 1969), p. 52.
68. *Ibid.*
69. Goode, p. 305.
70. Cited by Yang, pp. 150-151.
71. *Ibid.,* p. 151.
72. See Charlotte Bunny Cohen, "Women of China," in *Sisterhood is Powerful* (Random House, 1970), p. 407; and Yang, p. 151.
73. Yang, p. 151.
74. C.T. Hsia, "Residual Femininity: Women in Chinese Communist Fiction," *China Quarterly,* January-March 1963, p. 169.
75. Chin, "Family Relations . . . ," p. 105.
76. Yang, p. 154.
77. Goode, p. 305.
78. K.S. Karol, *China: The Other Communism* (Hill & Wang, 1968), p. 297.
79. Ruth Sidel, *Women and Childcare in China* (Penguin Books, 1972), pp. 83-84.

80. *Ibid.,* p. 390.
81. p. 145.
82. p. 154.
83. pp. 84-85.
84. Yang, p. 152.
85. Chin, "Mainland China," p. 427.
86. Moseley, p. 125.
87. *Ibid.*
88. Schran, p. 69.
89. Quoted by Stanley Rich, *New Republic,* January 5, 1959.
90. Salaff, p. 44.
91. *Ibid.,* p. 47.
92. Salaff and Merkle, p. 68.
93. Karol, pp. 173-176.
94. Committee of Concerned Asian Scholars, p. 269.
95. Sidel, p. 23.
96. Shelah Leader, "Mobilizing 'Half the Sky'," *Far Eastern Economic Review,* December 23, 1972, p. 16.
97. Salaff, p. 47.
98. Sidel, p. 25.
99. Committee of Concerned Asian Scholars, p. 270.
100. *Ibid.,* p. 288.
101. *Ibid.,* p. 271.
102. *Ibid.*
103. *Ibid.,* p. 282.
104. Sidel, p. 62.
105. Klaus Mehnert, *China Returns* (E.P. Dutton . Co., 1972), pp. 52-53. Such pay differentials are confirmed by many other observers. See, for example, Jan Myrdal, *The Revolution Continued* (Pantheon Books, 1970), p. 104; and Salaff and Merkle, p. 44.

106. "China Today: Report of a New Zealand Engineer," *Intercontinental Press,* November 5, 1974, p. 1272.
107. Hugo Portisch, *Red China Today* (Quadrangle Books, 1966), p. 59.
108. Barry M. Richman, *Industrial Society in Communist China* (Random House, 1969), p. 303.
109. These industrial comparisons, which are typical for other major industrial indices as well, are provided by Richman, pp. 644-645.
110. *Ibid.,* pp. 302-305.

111. *Ibid.*, p. 306.
112. Yang, p. 112.
113. Belden, p. 316.
114. Goode, p. 303.
115. Yang, p. 129.
116. *Far Eastern Economic Review,* November 21, 1957.
117. Salaff and Merkle, p. 48.
118. Franz Schurmann, *Ideology and Organization in Communist China* (University of California Press, 1966), p. 377.
119. Yang, p. 130.
120. Salaff, p. 33.
121. Myrdal, *The Revolution Continued,* p. 50.
122. Salaff, p. 35.
123. Sidel, p. 27.
124. Committee of Concerned Asian Scholars, pp. 273-274.
125. *Area Handbook for the People's Republic of China* (U.S. Government Printing Office, 1972), p. 141.
126. Chin, "Mainland China," p. 430.
127. Goode, p. 293.
128. Snow, *Women in Modern China,* p. 7.
129. *Ibid.*, p. 57.
130. Goode, p. 294.
131. Snow, *Women in Modern China,* p. 7.
132. Leo A. Orleans, "Evidence from Chinese Medical Journals on Current Population Policy," *China Quarterly,* October-December 1969, pp. 138-139.
133. *Ibid.*, p. 139.
134. Carl Djerassi, "Some Observations on Current Fertility Control in China," *China Quarterly,* January-March 1974, p. 54.
135. Karol, p. 181.
136. *Ibid.*, p. 305.
137. Salaff and Merkle, p. 32.
138. It is rare that such attacks on privilege are printed in the Chinese press. The publication of this letter with its veiled attack on Chung Chih-min's father would seem to reflect the current campaign to purge higher ranking military officials whose aggrandizement of power on a regional level poses a threat to the Mao faction of the CCP.
139. Merle Goldman, *Literary Dissent in Communist China* (Harvard University Press, 1967), p. 23.
140. *Ibid.*, p. 48.

141. Wilhelm Reich, *The Sexual Revolution* (Doubleday, 1945), pp. 78-79.
142. *Ibid.,* p. 157.
143. Leon Trotsky, *The Revolution Betrayed* (Pathfinder Press, 1970), pp. 151-153.